THE ETERNAL DOOR

(A Special collection of DIVINE LOVE poems)

By the late Fler Beaumont

Copyright © Andrea Beaumont, daughter/executor for the late Fler Beaumont 2021

First published by Busybird Publishing 2021

Copyright © 2021 Andrea Beaumont for the late Fler Beaumont.

ISBN
978-1-922465-46-7

This work is copyright. Apart from any use permitted under the *Copyright Act 1968*, no part of this publication may be reproduced, stored in a retrieval system or transmitted in any form or by any means, electronic, mechanical, photocopying, recording or otherwise, without the prior written permission of Andrea Beaumont and Publisher.

Cover Image: - Craig Sillitoe and *The Age* - Life - residence, S.J.Liistro

Cover design: Busybird Publishing, A Beaumont
Layout and typesetting: Busybird Publishing

Busybird Publishing
2/118 Para Road
Montmorency, Victoria
Australia 3094
www.busybird.com.au

Dedication

In honour of the inspiring poetic work of the Being Fler Beaumont (born Diana Mary Bates), who passed to higher life on 1st September 2019. It is a privilege to reproduce her 'Divine Love' poems, as they encompass her belief that God is imminent in all creation. She feels she was guided from Eternal and higher Spiritual Sources to write these verses.

'UBI CARITAŚ ÈT AMOR DEUS IBI EST': wherever truth, loving- kindness and love are, there is God also'.
(EARLY GREGORIAN CHANT. MONASTIC TAIZE COMMUNITY, FRANCE.)

There is nothing holier in this life of ours, than the first consciousness of Love. (Henry Wadsworth Longfellow)

And at the touch of Love, everyone becomes a Poet.
(PLATO)

With permission granted to Andrea Beaumont
by Fler Beaumont during her life-time for
this material to be published posthumously.
ANDREA BEAUMONT – DAUGHTER/EXECUTOR

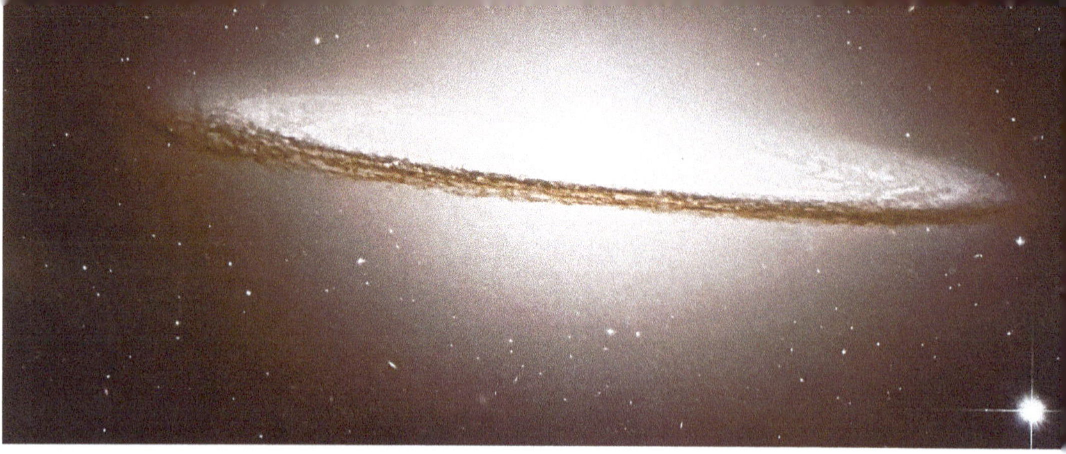

GOD

ONE ABSOLUTE

There is
One Absolute
Immutable Unknowable Unnameable
dwelling in its own
Perfect Unity.

From That
arose
the One Supreme God
source of all-that-is
Omnipotent Omniscient Omnipresent
all-loving all-compassionate all-forgiving

Whose divine rays
clothed by mankind
with many names, many attributes,
are Paths
that *all* lead back
to

the One Supreme God
Source of all-that-is
which arose
from
The Immutable Unknowable Unnameable
One Absolute
dwelling in its own
Perfect
Unity.

© DMB.FB. J. 21/01/18
Inspired by Iamblichus, Syrian Theurgist 3/4th Century

THE HOLY LIGHT

The Holy Light
of He who was to come
has cast its' presence
o'er the waiting world,

With arms outstretched,
embracing all-that-is.
Love peace compassion
now gently flow.

Joy awakens
from her slumber deep;
she gazes with pure rapture
upon the Holy Glow.

Heaven smiles,
Time has found her place
to welcome Home
the Hero from the Race.

The Morning breaks
with gladsome Song
as Freedom wakes
the ransomed throng:

Prodigals sons daughters
dark pale bright
now Love-enfolded
within the Holy Light.

© DMB. FB. J. 20-01-18

GOD'S CHURCH

Where is God's Church?
where does it shine
with glory, revealing
His Presence Divine?

Where is God's Church?
'Tis our planet Earth,
for He is the Presence
within it since birth.

God dwells within
man, plant & beast,
the mountains, the desert,
the great and the least.

Wherever we go,
wherever we meet,
'Tis God's Holy Church,
Divine & complete.

Whatever we share,
be it small or great worth,
we give to God's Presence
within Planet Earth.

So whenever we wish,
with God to be,
wherever we are
is God's Church, and it's free.

© Diana Mary Bates AKA Fler Beaumont 17-02-17

WHO SHALL SAY?

Who shall say
what is right or wrong?
Who will write a symphony
or a love-song?

Who shall say
if the gold is there
at the end of the rainbow?
Who will care?

Who shall say
that their song is true,
if the grass is green
or the sky is blue?

Who shall say
that the stars all sing
a song of joy
for the Cosmic King?

Who shall say
where it all began
before creation,
woman or man ?

God only knows
the answers, they say;
but we are all God
immersed in His Play.

© DMB/FB/J 5/5/12

GOD'S SONG OF LOVE TO HIS CREATION

Prologue
Ah, my beloved world of All-That-Is:
I have known thy night shimmering
climbed the waterfall of stars
beheld the splendour of thy universe,

swam in the Primal Sea,
leapt between great galaxies
merged with molecules atoms quarks
danced with Gods and demigods

gazed upon the beauty and the terror of your Being
rode the ocean's crested foam
laughed with the whirlwind
caressed the fragile cobweb

whispered with the leaves
gleamed in gems deep-hidden in the earth
rejoiced with flowers in the warm sunlight
played with moonbeams in the cool starlight

skimmed across tender blades of grass
kissed the smoothness of pebbles.
Ah, my beloved world of All-That-Is,
Let me sing my song of Love to Thee:

Song
The Unmanifest put forth three Planes,
the physical, Divine,
High and lower Spiritual.
Beyond them all was Mine.

Continued ..

I rode upon the Wings of Time
touched Creation's face
saw many Gods arise and fall
as Others took their place.

I witnessed newborn Planet Earth
erupt and fiercely grow,
the changing of the seasons,
sun and storm and snow

great beasts that trod the arid plains
the humble busy ant
the oceans and the shining seas
rock and worm and plant,

Mankind's blight and blessing
his ecstasy and grief
the Miracle of Nature
of root and bud and leaf.

I frolicked with the Autumn leaves
and through the mist I heard
the tinkling of the crystal stream
the song of breeze and bird.

I hungered with the homeless cat
drank the cup of pain
laughed with little children
wept with falling rain.

I joined you in your journey
my lovely wondrous World.
I saw and felt the whole of it
as slowly it unfurled.

Epilogue
I hold you all in my embrace,
Love clasping His Beloved,
together we share the Cosmic Dance
My wondrous World and I.

Let me kiss away your tears,
allay your fears,
and We shall dance forever
within My Light Divine.

In the final Consummation
the Manifest shall merge
with the Pure Unmanifest
and once again, I shall be whole.

I am One.

© DMB. FB. J. 20/3/11
(Channelled from God-Source)

GENESIS DIALOGUE

The snake gave an apple to Eve.
The next day, he said "I believe
that God told a lie
when he said you would die.
You still live! Tis the gods who deceive!"

God whispered softly to Eve
"Tis the serpent who tries to deceive.
You were immortal.
Now you are mortal.
My warning you failed to believe."

Eve replied with a faint hint of mirth,
"I've a question – for what it is worth:
If we <u>all</u> multiplied
And <u>none</u> of us died,
How could we all fit on Earth?"

"Ah, my child," God replied with a smile,
"You would only be there for a while.
I would raise you up here
to my Heavenly Sphere.
No more let the serpent beguile!"

The three of them all went their way
unto hostile land far away
where others they met
who had not sinned as yet,
the harsh price, like Eve, had to pay.

"Why not punish the one?" asked the snake,
"then the others your law will not break."
God replied, "I abhor
<u>your</u> voice evermore;
now a hiss is all you make!"

<u>This</u> God smites with cruel iron glove!
let us turn to the One far above
who wields no steel rod,
but <u>is</u> the <u>True</u> God
of peace, light, compassion and love.

© FB-DMB 2010

GOD IS THE PRESENCE

God is the Presence
indwelling all of His creation;
from Archangel to Ant,
from Galaxy to grain of sand.

He is the king on the throne,
the beggar on the street,
the eagle flying free,
the bird in the cage.

He is the pampered pet,
the homeless starving cat,
the fish trapped in a bowl,
the tortured lab-rat.

God looks out at us
through the eyes of our child;
and through the terrified eyes
of the lamb awaiting slaughter.

Whatever we do
to the least of God's creatures,
we do it unto *Him*.
And with that measure we mete,
so shall it be measured to *us*.

Therefore let us give peace,
comfort, freedom, love
to all creatures,
for God is the Presence
indwelling *all* of His creation.

© Diana Mary Bates AKA Fler Beaumont 04-02-18

GOD IS THE PRESENCE
(version 2)

God is the Presence
which dwells within us,
speaks softly to us.

God's breath forms life,
sustains the universe,
enfolds it in His Love.

Though sometimes blind
we cannot sense the Presence
not hear the voice of God.

Mankind has made our world
a fearful and dreadful place
in which to dwell.

Yet even in the chaos
God's Presence brings forth heroes
who shine within the gloom.

God gives the gift of Hope
to light our way
until a better Day is born.

God is the Presence
with remains within us
through good and bad times
and which shall guide us safely Home.

© DIANA M. BATES   AKA FLER BEAUMONT 22-11-18

GOD'S DREAM

He creates a world
of ephemeral beauty
lit by Dreams
sustained by Love;

where flowers bloom
wild birds sing
and rainbows paint the sky;
storms also rage
and in deep grass
wily serpents lie.

Time and space
make solid walls
which only Love can break;
till on that distant glorious morn
HE and Love AWAKE.

© DMB/FB/J. (2010)

HOLY ... HOLY ... HOLY

Beyond the realm
of Gods and men
came forth the One most Holy,
He spoke the Word,
The Great Amen;
Holy ... Holy ... Holy

Beyond the Night
came forth the Light
of He who wore the Crown.
From farthest Height
did He alight;
From Heaven came He down.

Holy ... Holy ... Holy
Beyond the Great Almighty,
came forth the Light
to conquer Night
with Sceptre burning brightly
Holy ... Holy ... Holy.

© DMB FB.J.   29-12-17

GOD SO LOVED THE WORLD

I walked,
head in Heaven,
feet upon the ground,
wearing the sandals of Creation.

Eternity was caught
within a moment rare;
Infinity
within a grain of sand.

And yet …
within that speck of time,
that grain of sand,
I found a love so great

That I chose
to share myself
to give of myself,
and fill that brave new world

with Promise of Eternity
to all
who choose to follow me
Home.

© DMB. FB. (01-11-17) J
Diana Mary Bates AKA Fler Beaumont

GOD'S PERFECT GIFT

In the beginning
God created Heaven:
power and might
radiant light
glory rare
beyond compare;
but …
something was missing.

Then
God created the angels:
shimmering wings
holy choir sings;
Lucifer sins
battle begins;
but …
something was missing.

Finally
God created <u>this</u> world:
garbed in clay
he showed us the way,
of himself he gave,
mankind to save.
This time …
nothing was missing.

© 2012 DIANA M. BATES AKA FLER BEAUMONT

REDEEMED: A WORLD IN CHAOS

I walk alone in Heaven,
Eternity is captured
in a fleeting moment in Time;
Infinity chokes
within a tiny grain of sand.

Where is the Great-Peace?
I know everyone,
but who knows *me*?
One tiny voice calls out
within the great cacophony.

Seasons intertwine,
Quarks run loose and free;
up is down and down is up.
Power is twisted into nightmares
in the hands of babes.

Road signs are lost,
songs are jangled,
leaves are twisted,
rivers run dry.
Where is Messiah?

Has Hope become
a garbled threat of war?
No, She sends
a golden ray of Light
to open the deadlocked Door.

I pour a cup of Love
upon the wounded World
and gently touch her forehead
with Redemption's plan.

The closed Cocoon shall open
when I'm born again;
and Butterflies shall fill the air
with gladsome Song.

Cacophony is gone
and Rapture tiptoes gently
o'er the field of mended Dreams.
A New Song fills the air
and Love is everywhere.

Eternity breathes again,,
Infinity runs free,
Heaven wears the Crown of Peace
and gentle Harmony.

Gone is the Glass of Darkness:
We know as we are known.
Maya is fled.
And God is on His Throne.

© DMB. FB. J. (9-11-17)

GOD'S TEAR DROPS

As He beheld the plight
of his beloved Planet Earth,
God's tear-drops fell
as the gentle rain:
cleansing
refreshing
re-vitalizing.

Would that God's tear-drops
also cleanse refresh re-vitalize
the minds and ways
of Mankind:
grown hard and callous
pillaging the Earth
and all Creation.

As the Pendulum
swings one way,
so it must swing back
the other way.
As ye sow,
so shall ye reap:
Such is God's eternal Law.

Let us leave the future
of Planet Earth
in God's fair hands
but also do <u>our</u> part
to stay the everflowing
tear-drops of Mankind
beast and environment.

© DMB. FB. J. (2010)

GOD BEYOND ALL GODS

O Beauty beyond beauty,
Love beyond love,
O God beyond all Gods,
beyond Heaven above.

'Tis thee do I worship,
Thee I adore.
Thou art the Power
beyond every law.

O Glory of glories,
Pure beyond pure;
all may vanish;
'Tis *you* who endure.

You create the Creator,
measure out time.
Thou art the One
beyond the Sublime.

O Holy most Holy
Might beyond Might
'Tis You who exist,
O Light beyond Light.

You are Reality,
we are your Dream.
Above and beyond all,
Thou art Supreme.

© DMB.FB.J (10-07-14)
© Diana Mary Bates – Also known as Fler Beaumont (2014)

GREATER FAR

The speck of dust looked up and saw the grass.
He said, "Oh lovely one, I'll worship thee."
The grass just sighed and said, "In time I pass."
Then she glanced up and saw the stately tree.

"Oh mighty one," she cried, "most surely you
must be the greatest power that could be."
The tree gazed up to see the sky of blue.
and claimed, "You are the One eternally."

The sky, in humble worship, watched the star
the shone so brightly in the sable night.
He said, "Oh radiant One, you surely are
the One above the all, the power bright."

The star gazed up and said, "I worship God;
for He's the One, the Holy One, most high."
But God just smiled, and gave a knowing nod,
and said, "I see a Greater Far than I."

Fler Beaumont © 1968

NO GREATER LOVE

As a child
God created many worlds:
games to play
lots of fun
but …
something was missing …

As a youth
God created Sphĕre Wars:
battles to win
lots of adventure
but …
something was missing …

As a man
God created *this* world
which He so loved
that He came down
gave His life
showed us the Way.

This time
nothing was missing.

© 2007 F.B.(J.)

GOD'S HOLY GIFT

This little Bird
Someone sends from above,
feathers sky-blue,
his nature, pure Love.

So fragile is he
that Heaven shines through.
the wind 'neath his wings
is Heaven-sent too.

Too fragile is he,
to touch earth and clay;
he lives on the wing
by night and by day.

Alone in his Kingdom,
his shadow, pure Light,
whispers around us
so gentle, star-bright.

His beauty awakens
the world from it's Dream;
compassion flows from him,
celestial Stream.

This little blue Bird,
sent from above,
is God's Holy Gift,
crowned with His Love.

Divine is his Mission
and far he may roam
till Pure Love's redeemed;
then God calls him Home.

(c) DMB.FB. (16/5/14) (inspired by) "THIS LITTLE BIRD" written by JOHN LOUDERMILK 1965. © Sony/atv acuff rose music. Licenced by Sony Music Publishing (Australia) P/L. International Copyright secured. All rights Reserved. Used by permission.

CRUCIBLE

The universe of time and space
quivered into existence
as God immersed himself
within the Crucible of creation.

Scyntillas of his infinite Self
revelled in the dance, as Gods breath
quickened into incandescent life
galaxies and bric-a-brac of space.

His journey flung him down
the long and torturous path of evolution
where he became hunter and hunted,
friend and foe, lover and beloved.

He was the pure bright air of Eden.
the sulphurous fumes of Hell,
the beauty and barbarity of Nature,
the agony and ecstasy of man.

He was the gentle breeze
that kissed the silver brook,
the howling wind that rudely ripped apart
the face of Nature in his fierce embrace.

To mankind God appeared as a man,
to beast as beast, plant as plant, rock as rock.
When God had experienced all-that-is
of time and space.

The universe finally dissolved
as an ephemeral dream,
and God, once again,
rested in solitary splendour.

©DMB.FB. (2012)

CRYSTAL STREAM

There's a crystal stream
where all creatures go
after they have left
the Earth far below.

It calms and cools them
removes any pain
that they have endured
in their earthly reign.

Birds' feathers are brighter
grass is more green;
lions and lambs
lie peaceful, serene.

Woodland surrounds them
and all their past friends.
love, joy and peace
and bliss never ends.

God walks among them-
His children so dear-
and never again
shall they know want or fear.

Each large and small creature
God holds in his arms
as the clear crystal stream
sooths, comforts and calms.

© DMB/FB/J 5/5/12

GOD'S IMMANENCE

It is written:

"In God we live
and move
and have our being".

God is immanent
in all creation.

Therefore,
in *us* God lives
and moves
and has *his* being.

© 2012 FB/J (Inspired by. ACTS. Chapt.17. V.28. St James Bible, Oxford Uni Press. London.)

FORBIDDEN FRUIT

Forbidden fruit hung temptingly
before Eve's eager eyes.
"Why place it there," she reasoned,
"if eating it one dies?"

The serpent slithered up to her
and said, "God tells a lie;
for on the day you eat of it
you surely will *not* die."

"Instead you'll gain the wisdom
of knowing wrong from right."
So, hearing this, Eve plucked the fruit
and took a hopeful bite.

She offered some to Adam.
Thus opened were their eyes;
they now became as God had feared -
astute, aware and wise.

In anger, God then cast them out
lest *they* eat of the Tree
of Life, and by this simple act
live on eternally.

Although God sent them down a path
of pain, they did *not* die;
the mind of man expanded,
reached far beyond the sky.

He now is Universal Superman,
no longer a mere brute;
and all because he dared to eat
of God's Forbidden Fruit.

© Fler Beaumont a.k.a Diana Mary Bates, 2004

7 HAIKU OF GOD

Winter night of stars:
God's diadem, brightening
our long darkest night.

Stars on a dark night:
God's glittering diadem
set upon the midnight sky.

Stars on a winter night:
God's glittering diadem
set upon the forehead of the sky.

Morning dew on the meadow:
God's gentle kiss
awakening His creation.

Early morning dew:
God's loving kiss and greeting
to His creation.

Bird in a small cage:
selfish cruelty, preventing
God's gift of free flight.

©DMB. FB. 2011 (J)

GOD'S SONG

From the Source of All-That-Is
came forth the Realm Divine,
the Spiritual, the physical;
Beyond them all is Mine.

I rode upon the wings of Time
touched Creation's face
saw many gods arise and fall
and others take their place.

I danced with gods and demi-gods,
laughed amid the storm,
swam within the Primal Sea
as galaxies were born.

I witnessed new-born Planet Earth
erupt and fiercely grow,
the changing of the seasons four:
blossom, sun, then mist and snow.

In the waters life arose
and on the land took form
till many species were evolved
to battle heat and storm;

great beasts that trod the arid plains,
the humble busy ant,
the oceans and the shining seas,
rock and worm and plant

Mankind's blight and blessing,
destruction and repair,
while all Earth's living creatures
watched, helpless with despair.

Now Man feels the vengeance
of ravaged Planet Earth
as floods and fires and earthquakes
herald a new Birth.

From the chaos and debris
a new world shall arise
like Phoenix from the ashes:
a bright new Paradise

where all shall live in harmony,
all creatures great and small;
for I shall dwell among you
because I love you all.

Then, when the world has run its course
and all have served their turn,
back to the Source of all-that-is
shall everything return.

Though Time and Space shall be no more,
yet in My Heart shall be
the world and all its creatures,
beyond Eternity.

© DEMB.FB. 24/05/11 Diana Mary Bates (J)
(DIVINE INSPIRATION)

I AM

I am all that exists,
the sunlight on grass.
I am all that is constant
and all that does pass.

I am the bird on the wing,
the small wayside flower,
the whispering wind,
the epoch, the hour.

I am the young and the old,
the rock and the beast,
time past, time to come,
the great and the least.

I am the atom, the world,
the silence, the song,
the fallen, the risen,
the weak and the strong.

I am morning and midnight,
Sorrow and joy,
I am dark and Holy light,
The man and the boy.

I am all that exists,
and all that is not,
boundless infinity,
the tiniest dot.

I am God, I am Devil,
I am Heaven and Hell.
Whatever exists,
or not, in me dwell.

© FB.DMB.J. (29-09-16)

LOVE OF GOD

God,
glorious Divinity,
you have the power
to create
sustain
destroy.

Behold!
you create love in my heart,
you sustain it
with your Divine Presence,
but …
it can never be destroyed;

for,
once the Lamp of pure love
is lit,
it is a Flame
which can
never be quenched.

Pure love is of God;
It is eternal.

©2012. F.B./J.

STAR-GENESIS

The One Supernal Source
of all that is
lay brooding
In the deep dark
mantle of night

Thoughts like a
shower of scintillating stars
issued forth
into the vast
reaches of infinity

Whirling twirling
swirling
until great galaxies
were formed
within which

A myriad glittering stars
danced joyously
as they marked time to the
celestial song of the sphēres

and the universe was born.

© DMB.FB (2010)

THE ANGEL OF DEATH

Death walks by with gentle tread,
love shining in his eyes;
he comes to us as loving friend
to gently loose earth's ties.

He pauses near the infant's cot,
he hovers near the bed
of tired and weary aged folk
to loose the silver thread.

His hand is cool and gentle
as he soothes the weary breast
and when the time is ready
he lays the soul to rest.

He's not the feared Grim Reaper
with scythe to cut us down
but a Being of great beauty
who rewards us with a crown

for all the tests and hurdles
we have passed on earth's hard road.
He leads us gently lovingly
to shed our heavy load.

He is the Being full of Light
who closes earth-time's door
to set us free upon the Path
of True Life evermore.

* * * * * * *

©Fler Beaumont a.k.a. Diana Mary Bates, 2004

BRIGHT BRIGHT ANGEL

Bright bright Angel, Angel bright
spread thy wings in blessed flight.
Scatter pearls of peace and love
Sent to bless from God above.

Calm the angry seas below
which o'er the land doth overflow.
Calm the angry mind of man
whom war and unkind deeds doth plan.

Let wild creatures live, be free,
birds to fly, fish in sea.
Let forests flourish, Planet Earth
recover from this awful dearth.

Bring enlightenment to all;
lift the overhanging pall.
Help mankind to mend his ways,
returning good and happy days,

Where children smile, birds can sing,
and peace and love bless everything;
where days are full of hope and cheer,
where air once more is pure and clear.

Let man and beast, all Planet Earth,
be aware of their true worth.
Bright bright Angel, Angel bright,
come bring God's pure Love and Light.

© Diana M. Bates AKA Fler Beaumont 04-12-18

5 HAIKU
(OF GOD & BIRDS)

Two birds on a branch:
Bright-winged angels in disguise
Singing praise to God.

The morning cock crows:
a sharp and short reminder
to acknowledge God.

The fallen sparrow:
noticed by God at all times,
and sometimes by Man.

Peacocks and lilies:
God's reminder that beauty
needs no additives.

Mopoke in a tree:
maybe God is watching us
not from a distance.
(or: and *does* give a hoot!)

DMB.FB. (2013)

9 HAIKU OF GOD to All

1
I am That I am
My unconditional Love
enfolds All-That-Is.

2
I am All-Knowing
All-Seeing and All-Present
I am the whole World.

3
My reason for Life?
to experience all things,
look upon Myself.

4
To man I am man
to creature I am creature.
to rock I am rock.

5
I dwell in your heart;
you live and move in my mind.
There is no Other.

©F.B D.M.B (2013)

9 HAIKU OF GOD to All (Page2)

6
How shall it all end?
you all return to my mind
and live forever.

7
Love is the true Gift
Of God to man, man to God.
Love is forever.

8
As I have loved you
please love ye one another
and *all Creation*.

9
I'll lead you all Home
with unconditional Love.
I am That I am.

HAIKU of All to God

All Praise be to God
In Him we live and we move
And have our being.

©D.M.B (Nov 2 2013) Fler Beaumont
(Last verse inspired by. ACTS. Chapt.17. V.28. St James Bible,
Oxford Uni Press. London.) & verse 8. JOHN. chapter 13. verse 34.

THE HOLY ONE

The Holy One is here.
He is the Presence,
the underlying Force
which binds
the fabric of the world.

He is the Love
unconditional,
forgiving,
which enfolds us all
in his pure embrace,

He is the Light
resplendent,
eternal and divine
which shines within
each speck of His creation.

He is the Breath of Life
which vivifies the whole,
the Spirit Divine
which dwells
within us all.

The Holy One is here:
the Presence,
unconditional Love,
Light divine,
Breath of Life.

The Holy One is here.
How blessed are we!

©DMB.FBJ. (7-11-16)
Diana Mary Bates

GOD IS ALL-THAT-IS

God is the Light of the World
the beauty and the Love
that surrounds us.

God's Spirit burst into Manifestion
and the Universe was born.

From the Star-stuff of himself
God became Mankind
all creatures
all leaf and rock
and all else beside

God's Love and Light
pervaded all.

We are the breath of God's Love,
We, the people,
and the creatures
and all that is.
We are God in action.

All was love and peace
And total harmony
until the wily Serpent
slithered in
planting the seed of Darkness.

To overcome the seed is to remember
God is the Light of the World
and His Plan will save us all.

©FB. (21-12-18)

SONG OF WATER

In the Beginning, I was there
When upon the dormant deep
God's spirit moved, as He awoke
The world from dreamless sleep.

I was the flood that cleansed the Earth;
The shimmering rainbow
That promised God's new covenant
To everyone below.

I parted as the Red Sea
To let God's chosen through,
And later baptised him who came
To bring a message true.

He walked upon my surface.
And, on a fateful day,
Pilate dipped his hands in me
To wash his guilt away.

I rush along as rivers,
Meander as a stream,
Cascade as mighty waterfalls,
And burnt-out lands redeem.

You hear me in the ocean's roar,
Yet in the brook I sing;
I am the gentle rain that brings
New life to everything.

Now that you've heard my story,
One thing I do implore:
Respect and use me wisely,
And I'll serve you even more.

©Fler Beaumont a.k.a Diana Mary Bates, 2004

ONE ABSOLUTE

ONE
ABSOLUTE
IMMUTABLE UNKNOWABLE UNNAMEABLE

…

From THAT
emerged
The GOD Supreme
Source of All That Is

…

His Radiance,
clothed by Mankind
with many names and attributes,

…

Each ray
Scintillating
with the golden thread of Truth
lighting each and every Path
leading back
to
The God Supreme
sprung from
ONE
IMMUTABLE UNKNOWABLE UNNAMEABLE
ABSOLUTE

©DMB FB.J. 29-12-17
Inspired by Iamblichus, Syrian Theurgist 3/4th Century

DAEMON/DAMON

FOR GOD MINGLES NOT WITH MAN. THE GREAT SPIRIT, LOVE, IS THE BRIDGE BETWEEN THE DIVINE AND THE MORTAL. PLATO'S SYMPOSIUM.

THE BRIDGE IS (DAEMON - DAMON - GOD, SPIRIT, PRINCE, ANGEL). OF DIVINE LOVE.

HYMN TO DAEMON
(GOD-IN-MANIFESTATION)

Your Divine Radiance
and Dazzling Darkness
permeates the universe
and I drown
in the rapture
of Your fathomless Beauty.

Stay, Daemon, stay!

Bless this fragment
of Your World
with one more
gleaming moment

leaving Your footprints
in the starry sands of Time

so that I may
follow You Home.

© Diana M Bates a.k.a Fler Beaumont (J) 2005-2011

DAEMON, THE STAR PRINCE

He descended
from his Kingdom of the Stars,
his beauty outshining the starry diadem
set upon the dark tendrils of his hair.

Translucent skin
lit from within,
eyes like the midnight sky
lucent with scintillating stars.

Grace beyond compare,
he raised one slender hand
and it seemed
that all the glories of the Universe

cascaded down
like a shimmering waterfall
of radiant splendour
blessing the ground whereon he stood.

His smile dispelled all fear,
Awakened unparalleled love and bliss.
The moment hung suspended
like crystal in the air.

When he left,
returning to his Kingdom of the Stars,
it seemed as though
all light had left our world,

yet…
upon the ground where he had stood
there lingered a soft shimmering glow
shot with glittering stars…

© DMB.FB. (2007)

TO MY BELOVED DAEMON
(FROM C.)

Emerging from the Tunnel,
you stood before me.
My heart moved so strongly;
I completely flowed to your side
Pledging my undying love.

We noticed Time
was never on our side,
our Love had barriers,
days turned into night.

In the darkness I called you name
as you were firmly imprisoned;
and I found your mind was free,
I felt your love beside me.

Finally, you were free at last.
The splendour of your everlasting smile,
dancing Star-eyes, I could see.

So many road-blocks once again
for you and me, and I sang,
"No matter what has happened,
my vow remains, my Love."

But now I see a future,
dazzling bright and wonderful to behold:
you and I, love, together everlastingly.

Time has come for us,
now we can be united,
together for ever and ever;
you and me, my beloved.

© (2012) A.B.

DAEMON
(TRUE BEAUTY)

Daemon, beloved Prince
from the Kingdom of the Stars,
your incomparable beauty
shines forth
upon the World.

Divine Prince
you are the True Beauty,
True Love
True Light
Of all-that-is.

As the radiance
of your beauty
and the power
of your Love
unite in Celestial Resplendence

the Stars begin to shine
with even greater Splendour
illuminating the Entire World.
We are truly blessed
By your Divine Presence.

© DMB.FB. 26/4/11 (DIVINE VISION & AWARENESS)

PRINCE DAEMON

From deep velvet night
shimmering with pure starlight
came whispering Angel Wing
bringing your everlasting smile.

When you alighted gently below
the world held it's breath
the sky-ground did glow.
We viewed for the first time
your divine and angelic presence.

From higher levels you descended
cloaked around; in tunnel dwelt.
We saw and heard you dimly
till one fateful Day released,
we saw you standing there.

Your eyes full of deep love,
inner joy, playfulness, and passion's glance,
drew all to your side completely
with one total thought in mind:
"How can I keep you <u>here</u>?"

Leaving the past and present
behind, my heart moved forward,
and I placed my hand
in yours, pledging my Love
to you, my beloved Daemon
Now and forever.

© 2011.C.TO DAEMON

MY LOVE, MY ALL, MY QUEEN

My love, my all, my cherished wife,

beloved and my Queen
you are the most beautiful
maiden I have seen.

Your hair so dark and lustrous,
heaven in your eyes
and when we are together
our two hearts harmonize.

Your hands are like two soft white doves
nestling in my own.
You touch, I tremble, and it seems
To Paradise we've flown.

The perfume of your lovely form
ignites me with desire
and as our lips meet in a kiss
my passion rises higher.

Your kiss sends thrills and shivers
right through me, and much more,
my heart is full of quivers.
Tis you whom I adore.

Your face and eyes, they thrill me
with rapture so divine.
To lose you now would kill me,
I thank God you are mine.

© DMB.FB.2001. Channelled from DAEMON to C.

TO OUR DIVINE DAEMON

From the beginning
the Immortal Light
sang a song of Divine Love.

It's purity and longing
sparked the Eternal River
to flow down
to all levels of Creation.

It drew all to hear
It's beauteous Song
and within it's crystal waters
your Divine face was seen.

Your everlasting Smile,
starlight eyes
and pure heart
made all who saw,
breathless in adoration
and wonder.

With one cry,
the word sprang
from each beating heart,
"I love you".

Then suddenly
your divine Presence appeared,
and the cry from all
reverberated Heaven ward
"Stay, our beloved Prince!
I love you".

©AB 14-02-17 Channelled from C. & all.

DAEMON

From the Divine Light,
He sprang forth,
a diadem of stars
glittering in his midnight hair.

Alabaster skin
lit from within,
Dark eye-mysterious pools of beauty
alight with stars.

Perfection personified,
slender grace,
unparalleled beauty-
Star-Prince Divine.

His gentle everlasting smile
concealed the steel within,
A charming Prince
from whom the fairy-tales took form.

The whole world fell in love with him.
But he was only lent a while
to reveal True Beauty,
awaken True Love.

Those Divine Beings
above and beyond the realm of God,
could not part with him
for long. And so he left.

As he returned to his Starry Realm,
the glow from his glittering Presence
bathed our world
in a shimmering radiance.

Reflected from his ethereal
transcendant beauty.
Daemon, Star-Prince Divine
had blessed us with a moment of Real Time.

© DMB.FB.J. 25.03.11 P.S.&A.+

HYMN TO DAEMON (1)

O lovely Prince,
You left your Starlight Kingdom
to join us and redeem us
on this mortal world below.

Beauty such as Yours
was never seen before
nor shall again.
Starlight in your hair
and in your eyes.

We fell in love with you.
Once seen,
never forgotten.

Though hidden for a while,
your Light still shone.
The shadows on the Wall;
they had their Dance

until you came again,
then we knew:
You are the One
the only One.

You are our Prince,
our Starlight Prince of Love.

© Diana Mary Bates (21-01-12)
Sophia to Daemon

HYMN TO DAEMON (2)

Daemon,
Your everlasting Light
sheds its halcyon rays
on a world
grown pale and dim.

Your revitalize
each wilted flower,
each troubled Soul.
They shine again for You.

There is no fear
when You are near.

You give the gift
of shining Hope
perfect Peace
purest Love.

Your scintillating beauty,
within and without,
enfolds us all
in tender Bliss.

You, we adore
forevermore.

© Diana Mary Bates (21-01-12)
Sophia to Daemon

HYMN TO DAEMON (3)

Prince of Heaven
blessed are we
that you have smiled
your everlasting Smile
upon our world below.

True Love came forth
when you descended
to light our world
with love and hope and joy.

You are the Fount
of all that's good
pure, true and noble.
Darkness is banished
when you are near.

Your starry radiance
is a pure waterfall
that cleanses
the specks of soot below.

From the ashes of Life
will rise the Phoenix
of Immortality;
and you shall reign
as Prince of Love and Light
from Everlasting
to Everlasting.

© D.M. BATES 21-01-12 (SOPHIA TO DAEMON)

HYMN TO DAEMON (4)

All the stars of Heaven
dance around your feet;
your scintillating Presence
makes the world complete.

You are every reason
why we all are here,
you <u>are</u> the Song of Love
ringing true and clear.

The flowers rise to greet you
and the golden Sun
puts forth his rays to tell you.
"You are the only One!"

The One who makes the stars to shine,
who makes the waters flow,
who lifts the wings of birds to fly,
who makes our hearts to glow

♡with love for you, Prince Daemon,
our Starlight Prince Divine,
for you alone, yes, only <u>you</u>
have caused the world to shine.

© D.M. BATES 21-01-12 (SOPHIA TO DAEMON)

HYMN TO DAEMON (5)

Divine Prince Daemon
your everlasting Smile
makes everything in our lives
joyful and worthwhile.

This little world of ours
is a far better place
ever since we gazed upon
your pure and lovely face.

There is truly nowhere
We would rather be
Than in <u>your</u> Divine Presence
now and eternally.

Your radiance and beauty
uplifts and blesses all.
with ever joyous hearts
we heed your gentle Call.

We'll follow you, Prince Daemon
to Heaven's golden Door
there to love and worship you,
our King, forevermore.

© D.M. BATES 21-01-12 (SOPHIA TO DAEMON)

HYMN TO DAEMON
(TRUE LOVE)

I have seen the night shimmering,
climbed the Waterfall of Stars,
beheld the splendour of Your Universe;

but *You* are more beautiful
than *all* of these.

Daemon,
You who are the Source of All-That-Is:
Creator
Sustainer
Destroyer;

Behold …
You have created Love in my heart.
You sustain it with your Divine Presence,
but …
You can *never* destroy it;

for
once the Lamp of True Love is lit,
it is a Flame
which can never be quenched.

I love, adore and worship You
now and Forevermore,
Divine Prince Daemon.

© Diana Mary Bates a.k.a Fler Beaumont (S & J) 1970-2011

THE LAMP OF TRUE LOVE
(A DIVINE VISION)

Daemon, Divine Prince,
Beauty beyond compare,
Source of all-that-is:

Behold!
you have awakened True Love
in all our hearts.

You sustain it
with Your Divine Presence.

Once the Lamp of True Love
is lit,
it is a Flame
which can never be quenched.

It is a scintillating Radiance
illuminating the whole World
leading us
to Eternal Bliss
and Beyond.

© DMB.FB. 26/4/11 (DIVINE VISION)

"AS DIATIMA THE MANTINAN SIBYL SAID TO SOCRATES".
"LOVE IS TRULY THE BLESSEDEST GOD, BECAUSE LOVE IS OF
THE EVERLASTING & IMMORTAL GIFT."

(PLATO'S SYMPOSIUM.)

THE LAMP OF TRUE LOVE (2)

Daemon, (God)…
You who are the Matrix,
Source of All That Is,
Creator
Sustainer
Destroyer;

Behold…
You have created Love in my heart;
You sustain it with your Divine Presence;
but it can never be destroyed.

For,
once the Lamp of True Love is Lit,
it is a Flame
which cannot be quenched.

Love is eternal;
It is of God.

© Diana Mary Bates
AKA Fler Beaumont (2012)

C.'S LOVE-SONG TO DAEMON

If I crossed the Sands of Time
and stood outside
your tent of Light
and whispered your name,
would you smile
and invite me in?
Yes, you would, my Love.

We would embrace and sing
and our LOVE.
would fill the Cosmos.
We would watch
the luminous moon
and diamond stars
gleaming in a dark velvet sky.

And if the Night Wind
tore me from your grasp
and I was hurled
through dimensions,
I would walk
the Tunnels of Time
till I found you again.
Yes, I would, my Love.

And finally,
coming to the Eternal Sea,
I would see you there
watching the ebb and flow
winnowing the Sands of Time
with your beautiful hands,
bathed in your Immortal Light,

"Lo, my Love,"
I would sing on the Shore,
"Here we meet again;
stretch out your arms
and embrace me,
my Love,
for Forever and Everlastingly.

I stand here
with my heart
in my hands
for You
my Love."

©. AB. CHANNELLED FROM C. TO DAEMON. 2011

MY LOVE

Roses are red
violets are blue
my beloved Daemon
I LOVE YOU

Young boy thinking
by black pool
looking for release
from tunnel cruel.

Time passed slowly
boy became Man
none saw within
Princes three interwovan.

Bursting forth quickly
you set alight
all the world
who gained flight.

To follow you
with outstretched heart
giving you all
body, soul, Songstart.

I am here
just for you,
in my hand
Red Rose True.

My love never
alters or wanes,
my heart here,
your side remains.

©ACB.2011   Channelled from JAY to DAEMON

MATRIX

Daemon/Damon
You who are the Matrix
of all that is

Creator Sustainer Destroyer

Behold
You have created Love in my Heart
You sustain it with your Divine Presence
But you can never destroy it

For once the Lamp of True Love is lit
It is a Flame
Which can never be quenched.

©F.B./J. 2017

JESSE'S LOVE-SONG TO DAMON
(Divine partners.)

I walk alone
Dripping with Divinity;
Endless Eternity,
Boundless Infinity.

But now, Eternity
is caught within a speck of Time;
Infinity is trapped
within a grain of sand.

You and I have become
as dancing Puppets
in the theatre
of our mind.

But *here*,
within Reality
we sift golden grains of sand
upon our Eternal Beach.

Love wraps us round
like a warm Cocoon
as Eternity prolongs,
Infinity expands.

No more I walk alone
for you, Damon, are here.
Our Worlds now merge
become Love's Perfect Sphere.

© DMB. FB. JESSE TO DAMON 18-11-17

DAMON'S ENCOUNTER WITH JESSE

I looked up with youth's eager desire,
glimpsing a great radiance
I became suddenly overwhelmed,
moving quickly to conceal
Now, I truly understand.

Suddenly the light was there

I touched His garment's hem,
He turned and looked at me.
I heard the Great Amen;
His brightness blinded me.

Now I see through a glass darkly,
but *then* I saw face to face.
That moment shall forever mark me.
I beg His forgiveness and grace.

My mind is still caught within it,
that rash reckless moment of mine
yet within that far reaching minute
I found a pure love Divine.

©DMB. FB. 05-08-18 (D)

THE HALLOWED GROUND
(version 2) (Damon's Love-Song to Jesse)

The hallowed Ground,
where Dazzling Darkness
clasps the Radiant Light,
awaits the tread
of the Beloved
as he emerges
from the sheltered Night.

We *both* must come
before the Morning breaks,
and the crystal Goblet
spills her wine
and another world awakes.

Awake! My Prince!
Awake! Come home.
Too long you sleep,
In Dreams to roam.

Heaven is the Home
where we both reside.
The shining Sea
may now be crossed
to the Other Side

where Love and Joy
are ever found
within the Realm
of Hallowed Ground.

© DMB. FB. D. 3/12/17 Damon to Jesse

THE STILL POINT

For one crystalline moment
I saw you…
gleaming white
in the Dawns bright light.

Plunging rapturously
down the crystalline Waterfall,
your black hair
spun with stars,
your delphinium eyes
eager for the day,
your limbs
like Grecian marble.

My breath caught
with the sheer beauty
of man and nature
entwined in that still moment.

And then…
like a burst bubble,
the moment broke…

and you were gone…..

© DMB/FB (2004) Laelon to Damon

AVE

Pure alabaster are her feet
And Heaven's on her brow;
Her smile lights all the many worlds,
The blossoms on the bough.

Her touch is as the gentle breeze;
O Maiden, chaste and pure,
Though all-that-is may fade away
her love would still endure.

Cometh all seasons, yet
The Fount remaineth clear;
The Waterfall of Stars reveals
release is almost here.

She wears the crown of Truth upon
her shining golden hair;
her step is light as thistledown;
so blest the morning air.

She is the Queen of maidens;
her Being overflows
with Love and sweet Compassion.
The world around her glows.

She's the Wellspring of all Wisdom
of Purity and Love
O Maid Divine most beautiful,
Guide us to above

Until we reach thy Portal;
"Ave!" shall we then sing,
for you are truly, surely,
the Heart of Everything.

© 2012 Prince Damon/Daemon to His Beloved Mãr 'e'
via D M Bates

DAMON

Day is bursting at the seams
But you are not here.

Through the mirror of my tears
I catch a glimpse
Of your Divine Radiance
dancing within the
droplets of sunlight

In the deep mystic shadows
beneath whispering leaves
I behold
the dazzling darkness
of your beauty.

My heart sings a song
of rapturous joy
because
you <u>are</u> still here.

©DMB.FB.J. (2000)

MORNING WAS BROKEN

Daylight
spilled in...
rudely
ruthlessly...
flinging photons
across the crumpled sheets
where you lay,
sprawled...
a Greek God

Tendrils
of gleaming black hair
kissed your pale forehead
as I kissed your silent lips,
breaking the spell...

and then...
you were gone...

©DMB / FB (2004) Laelon to Damon

DAMON'S DESCENT
(17-09-1998)

My beautiful beloved Wife,
since the Beginning of All-That-Is,
I have experienced a myriard of
exciting exhilarating adventures,
seen uncountable wondrous exquisite sights,
and thought that I was experiencing
supreme happiness and fulfillment;

But when I met you
and we fell in love,
the thrill and exhilaration
I felt in your embrace,
the breath-taking beauty
I beheld in your loving face,
and the supernal rapture
I experienced in our Love.

Only then did I truly
know and experience
sublime Joy and Happiness
and complete fulfillment.
Thank you for the time
we have spent together, my Love;
we can now enjoy the glorious Path
that leads to Eternal Bliss.

©DMB / FB 17/9/04. (DAMON TO C.)

A NEW-BORN WORLD
(Far, Far Down)

In the crystalline glitter of a New-Born World
I beheld the glow of your lovely eyes.
I reached for you- but you were gone.
I searched for you through Labyrinth of time.

For one brief moment I found you,
the rose-carmine cloak of Dawn around you
like a jewelled velvet gown.

Laelon's voice beside me whispered,
"Not yet, Damon, the time is not yet.
You have seen the Glow, held the Bloom,
Now you must descend, and find the Seed,
the Root from which they sprang".

Descending emerald mountains,
crossing iridescent rainbows,
leaping down crystal waterfalls,
I came at last
to a vast, deep dark Pool
with hidden depths.

Love impelled me downward,
down, down, down
almost blind;
other roots and vines
entangling me
blurring my vision
and my mind.

Far far down I beheld a wondrous sight:
a love-pink gem
glinting in the gloom,
more wonderous fair
than either glow or bloom,
yet all strung upon a single thread.

A maiden whose inner beauty
far outshone all others
was the Seed, the Root
for which the other parts came forth.

I touched you, and Love
burning brightly in our Tiger-eyes.
Yes, my Love, my Beloved,
we shall slink through the Velvet Night,
parting emerald grass
and drinking from sapphire pools
our hearts beating as one

Then shall we ascend
to the dazzling dark beauty
of my Matrix World where All began;
and from whence, you and I together,
shall leap with rapturous Love
to our eternal Future
and our Home.

©DMB / FB 30/6/04 (Damon to C.)

DIAMONDS

The universe is breaking up
my heart is breaking too
the stars are all dissolving
and the ground beneath my feet
crumples into dust.

No rivers flow
no birds sing
flowers droop their heads
and the darkness creeps
across the meadow.

Through the darksome gloom
your eyes shine into mine.
Daybreak leaps forth with renowed vigour
and the shattered crystal bowl
is whole again.

New songs begin
igniting the cosmos.
A rainbow tints the sky
as we ride the comet's tail
to the heights of heaven.

A fountain of new-born glittering stars
spills over us
and we are diamonds
          diamonds
              diamonds....

©DMB.FB.J. D+ (2012)

THE JEWELLED NIGHT

In the jewelled night
of the Dazzling Darkness
where my Beloved reigns
and weaves the endless possibilities
to an eternal Dance
of desire and experience,
my heart stood still when he smiled.

His graceful strength
belied his Sonic speed;
his infinite blue eyes
held the spinning Universes;
and his carefree laugh
sent the stars careening onto a new Path.

He held my hand
and nothing mattered
except that we were together forever.

Stay and be with me, my Love,
now and eternally;
and we shall slink
through the velvet night,
parting emerald grass
and drinking from sapphire pools.

But the joy and wonder
of our love will be
when our hearts lie together
beating as one.

© ACB. (2000) (C) TO DAMON

PASSION

My love for you
burns like a rose-red fire,
full of Passion's Wealth
and wild Desire.

I long to hold you
in my fevered arms
completely overwhelmed
by all your charms

So, be my Love
and I will swear to you
my Love eternal
constant, strong and true

that naught could ever
make me turn aside
from you my Love.
An overwhelming tide

of Love's fierce Passion
fills my yearning heart,
so fill my arms
and never let us part

© 19.02.11-DMB.FB. D-C

4 HEAVENLY QUATRAINS

(Daemon)

Starlight shimmering in the hidden pool,
ripples through to water's edge,
my heart joyously looks to Heaven's Door,
Saw your everlasting smile, Beloved.

(Justin)

Magnificent black Stallion with silver-steel hooves,
Dimly reflecting its Princely Rider,
He, Bringer of strength, my beautiful Love,
My Protector, your truth unveiled.

(Damon)

Damon of the dazzling midnight blue Heaven,
you spread your jeweled cloak,
Flashing your eternal proud stance, you dance;
My heart beats in love.

(Laelon)

Dreaming lilies, glistening beside the Enchanted Waterfall,
weave magical spells of you,
bringing your silvern hair, intense eyes, unfathomable
smile, deep into my heart.

©.ACB.14-15/6/2011

23 LOVE POEMS
written to my beloved Daemon/Damon between 1968 and 2006

1. I have known the night shimmering
2. From which night did you emerge?
3. Through the tapestry of stars
4. If I came walking through the stars of night
5. Day is bursting at the seams
6. One morning after we had bathed in sleep
7. The morning of our love woke quietly
8. When we walked in midday's field
9. Do you hear the pounding of my heart?
10. Beneath our bodies the rustling of leaves
11. You are my days in the sun
12. What would you do if I said I loved you?
13. I would capture all the stars of night
14. If I should touch the eagle in his flight
15. All we have done and said
16. I knew not why I loved the midnight sky
17. Before there was night or morn
18. Your love completes me
19. When shall we be together?
20. Your dazzling darkness permeates the universe
21. You are the world
22. For a while I was jealous
23. I melt into you

DMB.PM.FB. © 1968-2006. Inc pg 81-103

I have known the night shimmering
I have climbed the waterfall
of stars
I have seen your face
shining from the darkness
you who are darkness and the sun

Beautiful paradox

Absorb me and my droplet of water
but scatter me not down again
let me dwell within your self
I you, you me
let me beat with your pulse
overwhelm me dark beauty
with your oneness and
your love.

From which night did you emerge?
In what mirror was
your reflection cast?
Did night give birth to you
or did you give birth
to night?
Was darkness ever your image?
Did you bring forth stars
in the darkness of your eyes?

Your dark beauty shines
with lights more splendid
than a myriad of stars.

Are you night wearing darkness?
Or darkness wearing night?

I have only one request
Do not return whence you came
remain and light our darkness
with your light.

Through the tapestry of stars
I see your face
your eyes outshining stars
your hair beguiling night

I tremble with
unexpected joy

your breeze rustles
my feet of earth
my hair of grass
my hands of clay

I cry-"Remain!"
but you slip calmly away
to hide forever
behind the
cloak of eternity.

If I came walking through the
stars of night
and stood outside your tent
and breathed your name
could I then enter your placid
sleep of dreams
spin a dream within that web
and tip-toe out again?

Would your limbs stir
if I should touch you with my
dream?
Would your lips break apart
with words of love
if I should whisper in our dream
"I love you"
then go and wait outside
your tent for you to come
bringing your smooth ivory limbs
and warm lips with you
so we could share this
other dream
this waking?
I come
I enter
I await...

Day is bursting at the seams
but you are not here.

Through the mirror of my tears
I catch a glimpse
of your Divine Radiance
dancing within the
droplets of sunlight.

In the deep mystic shadows
beneath whispering leaves
I behold
the dazzling darkness
of your beauty.

My heart sings a song
of rapturous joy
because
you are still here.

One morning after we had
bathed in sleep
we dashed the crystals of night
from our eyes

some fragment still remained

unaware
it grew
even while daylight poured her
golden vial
until
by evening we were back
within our dreams

the fragment had become a tree

we plucked the fruit
drank deep the juice
and found forever after
we could not live
outside the tree
it was part of us
as we were part of it...

The morning of our love
woke quietly
as the bud opens
unfolding velvet fingers
to the sun's bright orb.

The first dew shone
like liquid stars
caught upon our parted lips

we shared a kiss
encompassing
all of heaven and hell
and found ourselves
spread upon the
camisole of earth.

When we walked in midday's field
the flowers breathed delight
and all the butterflies
danced upon the breeze.

Our hearts sang love
and there were
no more shadows
upon the earth.

Do you hear the pounding of my heart
when you are near?

If all the nightingales of the world
sang together
in one glorious celestial song
that moved the planets
in their course

If all the cicadas
were to shrill
until they raised
the roof of heaven

you could still hear
the pounding of my heart
when you are near.

Beneath our bodies
the rustling of leaves
applauds our love
overhead
the golden sun
whispers to the stars
that we are but
lent awhile
to teach the others
love…

You are my days in the sun
my morn of gilt
when golden light has
flooded
all the stones of night

my arms reach out
dazzled by your blaze
your eyes of living coals
your lips of burning fire

your finger-tips begin
a summer-storm

take me upon the
burning wind of your love
dash me upon your
stones of fire

but never let me be
without you.

Damon,
What would you do if I said I loved you?
Would you skim behind the canopy of stars?
Or fly away upon the summer wind?

And if I said my love would follow you?
Can any other thing outdistance love?

Then stay ,Damon, and weave your dreams
with mine
link them with threads of quicksilver
and jade
and let the crimson of my love
melt the dark image of your own.

I would capture
all the stars of night

weave them to a pattern
pure and free

and dangle them
upon the forehead
of the sky

there to shine and sing
and remind you
of my love.

If I should touch the eagle in his flight
could I fly too?

Beneath the winds of heaven
you fly high

I clamber up the tallest tree and call your name
the winds of heaven sweep my voice away
I stretch my arms and scrabble with my hands
to touch one feather
your eagle eyes gaze straight ahead
I lie upon the ground and weep
my heart rends itself in love for you

The tender threads catch at your feet
guide you down
and full of joy
I rest beneath your wing.

All we have done and said
all we shall ever do and say
has been done and said before

There was a time of formless love
before this element of time
grafted us to flesh and bone

We then were pure and more complete
as we shall be once again.

I knew not why
I loved the midnight sky

until I beheld
your dark hair
with its diadem of stars.

Before there was night or morn
or day
I walked with you
we gave birth to joy

Before there was tree or branch
or fruit
I tasted love with you

And now
before there is end or death
or long infinity
I am with you

We share it now…

Your love completes me

My love for you
- though it overflows
my entire Self-

is but a speck
in the infinitude
of your Divine Being

When shall we be together? I asked
you smiled and answered
we always were we are and always
shall be

But you are going away! I cried
Will you forget me then? you asked
I shook my head
I could never forget you, I replied,
you are in my thoughts forever
always have been always are and
always shall be

You smiled and left

I am happy that you are still
with me…

DAMON

Your dazzling darkness
permeates the universe
and I drown
in the rapture
of your fathomless beauty.

Stay, Damon, stay!

Bless this fragment
of your world
with one more
gleaming moment

leaving your footprints
in the starry sands of Time

so that I may
follow you Home...

© DMB.FB 2000

You **are** the world

therefore
I am forever
enfolded in your love.

For a while I was jealous
that other people saw you
that they too
could hear your voice.

I tried to block the path.

Then I realised
they see the sun
hear the birds
feel the wind
yet these three
heed them not.

You are seen and heard
but do not see nor hear.

I no longer care
who worships you

You worship me...

I melt into you
you melt into me

why is this whole
so much stronger
than either
you or I?

JESSE - DAEMON

"LOVE OVERMASTERETH ALL".
(VIRGIL)

I WALK ALONE

I walk alone
dripping with Divinity.
Endless eternity
Boundless infinity.

Countless eons roll.
I breathe a thought.
It solidifies
becomes a world.

It lives
and breathes awhile
then fades away
returns.

Countless eons roll
I breathe a thought
it solidifies
becomes a world.

It lives
and breathes awhile
then fades away
returns

I walk alone
dripping with Divinity
endless eternity
boundless infinity.

Countless eons roll
I breathe a thought...

© DMB. FB.   03-08-18   (JESSE TO C.)

TO THE DIVINE HERO
MY BELOVED JESSE-DAEMON

When the world thinks "hero",
they see battles with dragons,
and dangers overcome;
but little do they realize
the True Hero is amongst us.

Our Divine Hero,
coming to make our world easier,
and to bring us all safely home,
has had to face untold dangers,
inhabit a frail vehicle,
and found a high spiritual house
in turmoil
because of the Darkness.

Yet, he set about to clear it.
He gave love to the lonely,
money to the needy,
and befriended the outcasts
and lower-world.
All creatures were sacred to him,
and their well-being.

Yet none knew him,
and of his Divine Mission.
His cloak of young man,
his humbleness,
gave them grounds to be unkind,
but nothing swayed him
from his Path.

True heroism shines through
all his actions and plans.
His unselfishness is visible
in all his thoughts and deeds.

He is the Defender of Justice,
brave beyond compare.
He is the Divine Hero,
our beloved Jesse-Daemon.

I am in awe of you,
my beloved Boy
of golden heart and wing,
the True Hero.

I am blest to be beside you,
to help in every way I can,
and to know
our future will be together forever.

© AB 14-02-17
Channelled from Jay, Jesse's high spiritual Helper.

MY MANGER
(version 2)
(JESSE'S SONG)

I walk alone
dripping with Divinity:
no name, no number,
just... BE

The wild-bird in my heart
sings, "I must be free
to wing throughout Infinity,
sing through all Eternity."

Yet... I seek a manger
soft and sweet
where I may dream awhile
and rest my feet.

Forever's crown of Freedom
lies heavy on my brow
as present, past and future
all merge into the Now.

I find a gentle manger
flowing with sweet Dreams;
bear-like arms of love to soothe,
cool as crystal streams.

Still I walk alone
dripping with Divinity,
in endless Eternity,
boundless Infinity.

But now I have a manger
where I may rest awhile
wrapped in gentle bear-like arms,
and blessed by Love's sweet smile.

© DMB.FB. J (6-10-15)

THE VICTOR (JESSE)

He was an eagle flying high
struck down while in mid-flight
by fierce and fickle winds of Change,
his crown no longer bright.

He fell beside the Crossroads
of Hope and dark Despair
anger, pain, confusion
gripped his mind and left him bare.

As one door closed behind him,
a ray of light above
revealed another doorway
to unconditional love.

Hope and peace, forgiveness,
ignited once again
the noble eagle's strength within
to overcome his pain.

As his strength returned once more,
he chose the Road Divine;
he turned his back on black despair;
his eyes began to shine.

Again the splendid eagle flew,
his crown now burning bright.
The man he had become stood tall
- the Victor of the fight.

©B.T. Fler Beaumont a.k.a. Diana M.Bates 19-02-11

9 HAIKU OF JESSE THE ROOT

1
Jesse, the Root, says:
I have come to save your world,
to make it easy.

2
The Root is of God
who calls forth all Creation
like the daffodils.

3
The Promise of Spring:
when all springs forth once again
from the Hidden Root.

4
From the Root of God
spring forth all living creatures
into Creation.

5
The plant may wither
but because the Root endures,
it shall never die.

6
The Eternal Root
underpins the foundation
of the entire World.

7
As the Root endures
so does All ever remain
in the Heart of God.

8
Jesse is the Root
which shall save the entire World
with Love forever.

9
There's Divine Wings
descending from Heaven above
and its name is Love.

© DMB. (Nov 2 2013)

JESSE, THE ROOT OF THE TREE OF LIFE

Deep within the Absolute
dwelt a Being in the Root,
full of love, compassion light.
All at once his mind took flight.

From his heart burst forth a Tree
of Life and Love and true beauty.
All was perfect and serene,
but *active* Life could not be seen.

He put a speck of dust within
the tree, so action could begin.
He longed to play, to have some fun,
which could not be with only one.

The speck of dust began to stir
and other life-forms did occur,
some good, some bad, some dark, some light
within the tree did they alight.

Soon began a Battle royal,
and Jesse had to fight and toil
A bitter journey then ensued
as Jesse fought a deadly feud.

But full of Love, compassion, light,
Jesse won the dreadful fight.
He rescued all the good and pure,
all whose love did still endure.

The dust, now beaten, disappeared
and Paradise at once appeared.
The Stranger, Jesse, was now known
and took at last his rightful Throne.

He then bestowed a Holy Kiss
awakening true and joyful Bliss.
Never more would Jesse roam,
for he had found his own true Home.

© DM. FB 17-09-18 ♡ Channelled from above P.S & B.to J.
DIANA MARY BATES - FLER BEAUMONT

JESSE'S SONG

Like the all knowing Lizard;
I know everything;
I know everyone,
but they don't know me.

Like the Lizard,
I stand perfectly still
like the wet brown leaf
of a fading Autumn Day

while my eyes,
twin sparks
Sprung from Time's Eternal Flame,
See the world going round.

They have seen the Beginning
and the End;
but I enfold it all
within my Silence.

Though the Secret is in my Silence,
I can't stop talking;
but the Secret
remains hidden within my Silence.

© DMB.FB.J.(9-4-14)

JESSE'S JOURNEY (REDEMPTION : TIME)

I rode the Crest of Heaven's Wave
Then plumeted to Hell's deep cave
The mirror cracked

I rose again, unbridled, fierce and strong
And sprang upon the World's Wild Carousel.
Round and round
Up and down
Till bruised and beaten I wept alone
within my darkened Cave.

One thin stream a ray of Light
pierced the gloom.
Redemption whispered in my ear
"Tis Time."!

Straight way up I rose upon that Thread of Light
that led to Heaven's gate.
Home at last.

But far below, my Brother called.
I could not turn away,
but once again lept down to Hell's dark Tomb.

"Stay, stay."! my Brother pleaded,
so I played the game.
As he played the "Check"
I played the "Mate" of Love
which caught him unawares

He wrestled and we blended
Black into White

White into Black
until the Cloak of Love
Ignited all our Dreams
of Yesterday.

On the golden Wings of Love,
like two shooting Stars,
we sped above
where Heaven's Gate stood open
shining bright.

Not one, but two lost prodigal Sons
came home.
The mirror United.

        One Yoke
        One Son
        One Song
        One Throne
        One All
        Light
        Love
        Peace

        Unity

        Lux-Pax

© F.B.J. 21/1/11

JESSE AND THE ONE ABSOLUTE

BEFORE ALPHA,   BEYOND OMEGA

BEFORE ETERNITY, BEFORE INFINITY

BEFORE AND BEYOND

ALL   POWERS
       FORCES
       GODS
       ALL-THAT-IS

I AM

NEITHER LIGHT NOR DARKNESS

NEITHER GOOD NOR EVIL

I AM ALL OF THESE AND MORE

I AM

THE SOURCE OF ALL THAT IS

I AM

ABSOLUTE

FROM THE ROOT OF MY BEING

THROUGH THE HEART OF MY BEING

CAME FORTH

JESSE

CREATOR OF ALL WORLDS

THE ONE

WITHOUT WHOM THERE IS NOUGHT

HE IS

THE DIVINE DREAMER

WITHIN WHOSE DREAMS

ALL WORLDS ARE BORN

ALL BEINGS LIVE

ALL POWERS DWELL.

HE

ALONE

BEGINS AND ENDS

THE

DIVINE DREAM

AND THEN

UNITES

WITH

THE ONE ABSOLUTE

© DMB.F.B. 2010/2014 (Divine Awareness)

LOVE

"LOVER, TAKE MY HAND, REACH AGAIN
INTO THE YEARNINGS OF ETERNITY.
THERE YOU WILL FND ME WAITING
AS EVER, TO CLASP YOU IN MY LOVE."
P.MARDON

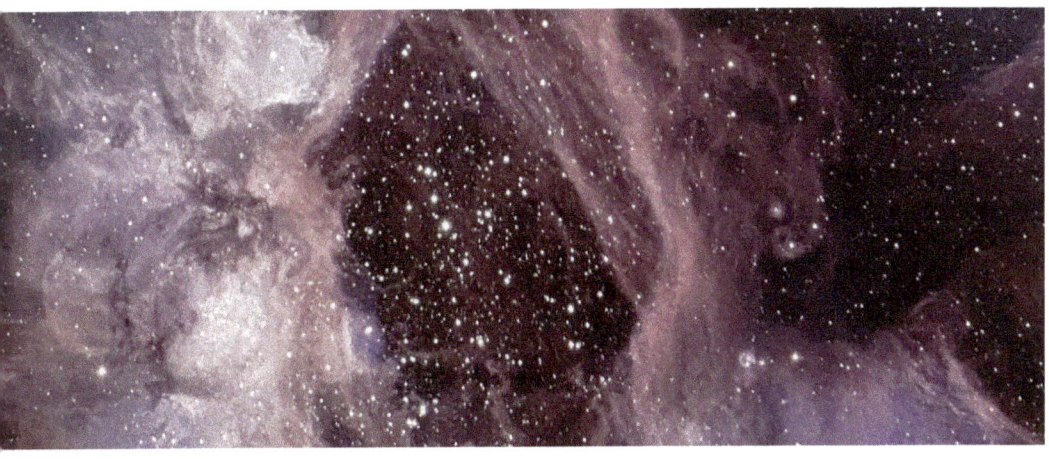

THREE LOVE POEMS FROM JESSE TO CHIA
NO 1

TOGETHERNESS

There are no words
in any language
to describe the depth
and the breadth
of my love for you.

Many people who love
need spaces
in their togetherness.

But I long to be
in *your* presence forever
with no spaces.
This is my greatest wish,
my most fervent prayer.

So, let there be no spaces
in our togetherness,
my dearly beloved.

© DMB.FB.J TO C.10.35PM   24-04-16

**THREE LOVE POEMS
NO 2**

THE JEWEL OF LOVE

My love for you
is like no love
that has been
or will be again.

It shines forth
from the core of my being
like a beautiful gem
unique and timeless.

It is beyond the value
of all that is;
and I know
that it's twin-gem
shines forth for me
from the centre
of your loving heart.

Beloved, we are truly blessed
to bear this love
so pure and timeless
each for the other

We are each other's Heaven,
crowned with Perfect Love.

© DMB.FB.J TO C.(11PM.)   24-04-16

THREE LOVE POEMS
NO 3

THE VICTORS OF LOVE

Our love had no beginning,
it will have no end.
It forever was
and forever shall be.

We have witnessed many worlds
come and go,
weathered storms and sunshine,
travelled many paths.

I have wept to see
the terrible tests
you have endured
to prove your glorious love.

And I have conquered demons
on my own torturous path
for love of you.
We both emerge the Victors.

Now, behold-
a new dawn breaks!
We stand upon the cusp
of a bright and gentle road.

So, take my hand, my love,
and walk this road with me
to our home of loving togetherness,
for all Eternity.

© DMB.FB. J TO C.(5AM)   25-04-16

A LOVE SO GREAT

I walked
alone in Heaven
as in a dream
of perfect peace.

I looked upon Eternity
I gazed upon Infinity;
My own reflection
gazed back upon me.

I captured Eternity
in a moment of time
and Infinity
in a grain of sand.

In that fleeting moment
within that speck of sand,
her smiling face
gazed back at me.

I found a Love so great,
so beautiful, complete;
it's glorious Radiance
put the Universe to shame.

It shone upon me,
fuelled by Love,
refreshing my soul,
making me whole.

We walk together
in joy supreme
in Highest Heaven,
This is no Dream.

© 7-11-17 DMB.FB.J.To C.

THE HALLOWED GROUND

The hallowed Ground
glittering with gems
cloaked with Light
awaits the tread
of the Beloved..

The Spirit and the Bride
must come
before the Morning breaks
and the crystal Goblet
spills her wine
over the waiting Day.

Awake! My Prince,
too long you sleep.
The Bride has risen,
her tryst to keep.

Heaven awaits the Victor,
joy awaits the Bride.
The shining Sea
may now be crossed
to hallowed Ground
where Love and Peace abide.

© DMB. FB.3/12/17 (JESSE TO CHIA)

SPRING HAS WAITED

Spring has waited for us, LOVE;
She walks beside us hand in hand.
Together now we share a better world,
a joyous Springtime Wonderland.

We share our food in sunshine bright
and know the success is ours fore'er.
The woodland is blessed by Holy Light,
peace and joy and love are everywhere.

You are the one True Love within my life
and I shall live my life for only you.
You'll be my one beloved wife
as now we share a love so pure and true.

So take my hand and walk fore'er with me.
The Storm has passed and Love is all around.
Together shall we share Eternity;
At last our Springtime joy we've truly found.

CODA

"We encircle each other's hands
through seasons of time,
we will always have each other."

©DMB.FB.21/9/14
Channelled from Jesse to C.

ALCHEMY

Dashed are the dreams
of yesterday.

You took the shards
and scattered them
as stars
across the mantle
of the night.

And Lo!

My world was filled
with hope
and love and joy

and never-ending Light.

© 2003 DMB-J

MORE
(SINCE YOU CAME)

Since you came into my life
there are more songs to sing,
more flowers in Spring,
more birds on the wing.

Since you came into my life
there are more stars in the night,
more colors, more bright,
my step is more light.

Since you came into my life
there is more joy to share ,
more hope everywhere,
more love in the air.

Since you came into my life
each morning I greet
the new day so sweet.
My life is complete
since you came into my life.

© DMB.FB.J. (2011)

MY SONG OF LOVE

My love for you has no limits
no boundaries
it spills beyond Infinity
reaches beyond Eternity.

There is nothing I would not do
for you, my Beloved,
no path too hard to walk
no mountain too difficult to climb.

Your love fills my heart,
my Soul, my Being
with so much hope
and Light and Joy

that I would shower your days
with rainbows and butterflies and bird-song
and fill your nights
with moonbeams and starlight and sweetest dreams.

I will follow you, my Beloved,
where'er you may go
be it in Heaven above
or on Earth or Hell below.

It matters not
what the future may bring
for when I am with you
it is eternally Spring.

©DMB.FB.2007
Channelled from J to JC

TRUE LOVE

I have seen the Night shimmering
climbed the Waterfall of Stars
beheld the Splendour of the Universe

but *your* love is more beautiful
than all of these.

Your love is deeper than the Night
more radiant than the Stars
more constant than the Universe.

Your love is warmer and more gentle
than the Summer breeze
sweeter than all the flowers
in Spring.

Your love encompasses
every good and noble quality
it cleanses and refreshes
my Soul.

If there were no other reason
that the universe should have existed
it is this:

that you came forth
from the heart of its Being;
for you are true Beauty,
you are True Love.

© DMB.FB.2007
Channelled from J to C

DAEMON'S LOVE-SONG TO CHIA

Fairer far than any flower
more radiant than a star
jewel most precious in my Crown,
My everything-you are.

Heaven is in your lovely eyes
you touch is utter bliss
and I could drown forever
in the rapture of your kiss.

Beyond the reach of Man and God,
my adoration grows.
Where this most glorious path may lead,
only Heaven knows.

Infinite my starry realm
Infinite my love;
so take my hand and walk with me
through wondrous worlds above.

A thousand, million angels sing
to praise your beauty rare.
your pure eyes shine with love-divine
and midnight is your hair.

How blessed am I to win your love,
to know you are my Queen.
You're my Alpha and Omega
and everything between.

You have my heart and all I am,
my one and only Love;
thus shall we dwell forever
in Infinity above.

© F.B.D. 2010

JESSE'S SONG TO C.

Midnight curls around us
as we lie on golden sand
our warm young bodies glistening
caressed by ocean's hand.

The glitter of far-distant stars
entangled in your hair.
whisper of a love so deep
few lovers venture there.

Your love swiftly sweeps me
to a realm of perfect bliss
as at last we share the rapture
of a long-awaited kiss.

My love for you, ignited
by passion's holy fire
is a flame which never can be quenched
but ever lifts us higher.

Our bodies and our loves entwine
to take us to a world divine
where I am ever yours, my love
and you are ever mine.

© 2018. FB/J-C.

JESSE'S SONG TO C.
(NO 2)

My Beloved
you are fairer
than all the flowers in Spring,
brighter than all the stars
in heaven,
More precious than all the jewels
in the world.

Your love
is my most treasured gift;
and never shall I leave
the circle of your wondrous love.
My love for you
is forever, eternally and Beyond.

©2018 FB/J-C

DAEMON (TO C.)

HAIKU

Like a shooting Star
I dance beyond God and All
in the Real Cosmos.

POEM

I behold the Absolute
but it sees not me.
I dwell Beyond-It-All
in the Real Cosmic Sea.
I sent a kiss on silver wings
down to my chosen Love
and whispered to her "you're my Queen;
please join me here above".

I came down on silver wings
and *you* walked up to me,
and said you'd be my true Star-Queen
everlastingly.

And now the End is very near,
they play their Wicked Game;
but we shall go together
our Future to reclaim.

So take my hand, Beloved,
On silver Wings we'll rise,
they'll bear us both to safety
beyond God's highest Skies.

© FBØ-C.2017.

YOU

You turn on my sun
and light up my stars.
You make smooth my path
so no pebble jars.

You teach birds to sing
and flowers to bloom.
You open the window
and light up my room.

If you were not here
my eyes would rain tears.
My life without you
is the worst of my fears.

I'd brave every storm
to be where you are.
In every dark night
you are my star.

No desert's as hot
as my passion for you,
yet my love is more tender
than early morn's dew.

This poor Planet creaks
with its woe and its pain,
but one touch of your hand
makes it live once again.

I hope and I pray
that we never shall part,
for I've found my Heaven
in your arms and your heart.

© DMB-J (19-02-12)

7 HAIKU OF MEMORY

Memories of you:
a gently-flowing river
sparkling with jewels.

Memories of you:
a beautiful garden-bed;
not even one weed.

Memories of you:
a lovely sun-lit garden
fed by rain and tears.

Memories of you:
rainbows, butterflies and Song
beneath clear blue skies.

Memories of you:
Exquisite crystalline stream
lit by matchless Love.

Memories of you:
a splendid poet sparkling
with enchanting words.

Memories of you:
Queen of Poets charming us
with words of Pure Love.

© DMB. FB.J-C JUNE(2011)

THE BELOVED

The Beloved lay sleeping
awaiting the Kiss
of he who was to come.

Riding the wild Carousel of Dreams
she became
Queen and maid
friend and foe
lion and lamb
sun and shade
storm and calm

Yet she herself
was untouched by all of this
- chaste and pure.

Sometimes in her Dream
she would catch a glimpse
of the Prince of her Dreams
on the far horizon
and one special moment
she felt the silken caress
of his Kiss
upon her forehead.

She smiled
and stirred
knowing he was the one
who was to come.

Aeons passed
worlds come and went
still she slept.
Then
when he had fulfilled
his Divine Quest
he came
to where his Beloved lay
and his long-awaited Kiss
awoke her to Reality.

Lover and Beloved
rose again
never more to be parted
but to share
their Love Divine
through all Eternity
and Beyond.

© F.B.(DMB) 26-04-10 (J-C)

FLIGHT

I come to you
across the stones of night;
together do our winged souls
take flight.

The stars become entangled
in our hair
as wild winds sweep us
to Enchantment, where

sweet music draws us
to a Cosmic Cave
where you are Queen
and I your humble slave.

In adoration
place I at your feet,
gifts of lilies,
cherry-blossom sweet.

I sing to you
an Elven song of Love
while gentle moonbeams
filter from above

Then do our souls
entwine in winged flight
returning Home
across the Stars of Night.

© 19.02.11-DMB.FB.L-C

"MY BELOVED HAS LONG SILVERN HAIR"

My Beloved has long silvern hair
that exquisitely gleams.
His protective white hands,
so pure and strong,
belie his quickness and Merlin Mind
that speed this Being through this time.

The wild swans answer his summoning call,
while the stillness of a green forest pool
reflects in his luminous eyes.

I cannot believe what drew him
to look in my direction;
and now to know
that he loves me too,
brings a well-spring of quivering emotion
and a rush to hold him for evermore.

Over the bridge of Dreams
you flew
to experience with your eternal Partner,
and now that we have met,
touched, love-joined,
our lives will be, my Love,
forever and endlessly entwined.

© .ACB(2006) (C to Laelon)

5 HAIKU OF LOVE
(5, 7, 5 Syllables)

Chi to Chia:

Chia, Beloved,
you are the whole world to me.
How I do love thee!

Jesse to C.

C. my true Love,
you're the wind beneath my wings.
How my Spirit sings!

Daemon to C.

C. my gift is
my everlasting True Love:
a gift from Above.

Jesse to Jay

My wonderful Jay,
you are the Light of my life,
all I ever need.

Daemon to Jay

Jay, you won my heart;
you were there right from the Start.
We shall never part.

©16-10-2013(FBJ.)(*1*)

5 HAIKU
(Daemon to C.)

C. shining bright,
your radiance sheds new light
on my Star-Kingdom.

Your Love lights my World
and all the stars shout for joy
because you are here.

C. (which means "bright"),
you are the most beautiful
of all Creation.

My Kingdom is bright,
scintillating with your Love
like a rare diamond.

How do I love thee?
Beyond the height, depth and breadth
of *all* Creation.

© DMB.(Nov 2013) *D.*

MY QUEEN

We came down from on high,
born of true Love and Bliss,
my Love and I;
we shared a pure kiss.

"My darling," I whispered,
"I'll make us a Dream
wherein I'll be King
and you'll be my Queen.

It will be our own world
of joy, love and light,
Springtime and beauty,
and gentle starlight."

No sooner we entered
than Darkness crept in
casting her shadow
of evil and sin.

Dashed were our plans,
right from the start.
Swiftly the Darkness
flung us apart.

But Love is far stronger
than evil, and so
we found each other
again, far below.

Now swiftly we'll rise
to our true Home above,
forever to share
our lives and our love

©DMB FB.J. 17-01-17

JOURNEY'S END
(CHANNELLED BY JESSE)

The universe has become
a small glowing candle
in a shadowed corridor.

Memory is far-flung
upon the shifting sands
of time,

which await the ebb and flow
of Mother Ocean's
tender Call.

I walk,
not trailing clouds of glory,
but bearing a tiny blue flower
the gift of Creation.

The candle flickers and goes out.
The universe becomes
another grain of sand.

The mask and cloak fall away.
I am Myself
once more.

I walk, bearing the tiny flower,
to find you waiting
on the Golden Shore.

I take your hand
and lead you
to a world of Light and Love
forevermore.

©3-11-16 DMB FB.J.

THE WINGS OF THE MORNING

The wings of the morning
folded around my shoulders
as daybreak awoke
from her dream
ushering in the day.

You are here to share my morn.
Joy burst into song,
doors long shut were open.
Your hand in mine
we can climb
the mountains of our imagination.

The golden dream we shared
rushes toward us;
it is real.
The storm is over,
the long wait is at an end.

The wings of the morning
are warm and full of love.
We have weathered the storm;
the best has come.
Your hand in mine,
we have won.

©DMB.FB.J 15-05-2016.

JOLYON'S SONG TO JULIETTE

I rose as a star of the morning
golden wings bearing me
along a path glittering with gems.

Great galaxies whirled on by
golden doors slowly opened
revealing you, my Beloved.

Your saffron robes
flooded the universe with golden glory;
a cluster of stars nestled in your hair.

Your beauty streamed forth
like celestial music
enchanting my heart and mind.

You are my Angel of Love
pouring yourself
upon my weary soul

I reached for you
"Not yet!" you smiled,
"But soon."

Continued...

We lay upon
the smooth white stones of Time
wearing our cloaks of Earthly pilgrimage,

Knowing that when the Wheel
has turned
one more time

We shall be THERE
to share our Love
forever and beyond.

© Jolyon DMB. 2012

JULIETTE'S HAIKU TO JOLYON

You were ABELARD

I was HELOISE

our love, ETERNAL.

©ABJ·2012

BRIDGE OF DREAMS

I came to you
across the Bridge of Dreams.
You love the Prince
and I love him too.

And yet... and yet... and yet...
when our eyes met,
Love ignited
passionate and true.

We shared a kiss
immersed in total Bliss;
the World existed
just for me and you.

I love you with my heart
and mind and Soul,
for your love brings me Joy;
it makes me whole.

And thus does Endless Love
enfold we two.
Across the Bridge of Dreams
I come to you…

© DMB/ FB (2004)   Laelon to C.

QUEEN OF MY HEART

My Beloved
you are the Queen of my heart.
I am enraptured
with your exquisite beauty
of Soul and Being,
your lovely face,
the purity of Love
glowing in your eyes.

I long to caress
your long dark shining hair.
Your slender form
melts into my own
as we are overwhelmed
by Holy Passion's Fire;
Love ignites between us
in incandescent glory.

Your playful and engaging ways
bewitch my very Soul.
Your peerless virtue
and incomparable loyalty
broke through my silent reserve
and lit my inner Sanctum
with a Love
beyond all loves.

My own dormant Love awoke
and knew with Divine certainty
it had found its joy Supreme
and True Beloved.

I love, adore and cherish you,
my lovely lady
Together we shall journey
to heights of Love Supreme
where Bliss and Beauty unsurpassed
await us in that Glorious Realm
which is our Eternal Home.

I give to you,
my pure and beautiful wife,
my constant and Endless Love.

© DMB/FB (21/06/04) LAELON TO C.

TO JAY

Never was man
more brave and true,
more warm and kind
than <u>you</u>, Jay, <u>you</u>.

A loving heart,
a helping hand,
one who'll always
understand.

You bring the sunshine
to my life,
and banish
all my woes and strife.

Battling on,
whate'er befall,
no matter where,
you heed my call.

No words describe
my love for you.
To you dear Jay,
I'll e'er be true.

© 3-12-10 F.B.-J.

TO CJ

You are the fairest flower
the brightest star in my sky,
you've given me Heaven here on Earth
and wings with which to fly.

You are truly all I could ever need,
you are everything to me,
you are my world, my dearest Love,
my whole Eternity.

Dear CJ, you are the one
who has truly illumined my day,
you chase the dark clouds out of my life
and bring Heaven on Earth my way.

What you have done for me, my love,
no-one else has ever done.
you are the brightest Light in my life,
my heart you have truly won.

There'll never be another
as dear to me as you.
no other love but yours could be
as constant and as true.

My love for you is constant,
it burneth bright and pure;
My love for you shall never fade,
it ever shall endure.

So take my hand and we shall walk
together evermore.
Your love and beauty outshine all else.
Tis you, I forever adore.

©15-12-12 DMB. FB.TO CJ.

YOU ARE MY HEAVEN

You are my Heaven,
my gift from above,
and all that I need
is your beautiful love.

Your smile brings a song
of Joy to my heart;
I'm where I belong:
a star-bright new start.

One touch of your hand,
sweet Rapture takes wing.
We're in a New Land
that's forever Spring.

The love in your eyes
brings Heaven to me.
Now Bliss ever lies
in my heart endlessly.

Your beautiful presence
brings joy to my Soul.
You are Love's very essence.
With you I am whole.

I never am alone
with *you* beside *me*.
My love's just for you only.
I shall ever love thee.

© DMB. FB.J to C 29-08-15

JAY, MY PRINCE
(A POEM FROM ABOVE)

There's been no man,
before or since,
to match your love,
your strength, my prince.

Yes, prince you <u>are</u>
to me, my Jay,
you help, protect,
in every way.

You are so loving,
brave and true;
no-one has done
as much as you.

You like to play
the bumble bear;
and in this game
I, too, can share.

We've shared a lot,
of pain <u>and</u> fun;
but when this weary
journey's done,

We'll both awaken-
joy supreme!
Free from this
shared Time – Space Dream.

© DMB FB.J. 17-01-17

TO MY BELOVED JESSE-DAEMON

Your Love alights on me
as soft as a butterfly,
warm, undying Love,
wrapping me in its' Divine arms.

There are no words
to tell you
how deeply I feel,
how blest I am,
that you have found me again.

When we dream,
we are together,
dancing in the meadow grass,
sunlight softly on our face,
the birds singing songs of Joy.

Our Day has come, my Love,
because we are here and there,
always together,
and forever.

© AB 14-02-17 Channelled from Chia

OUR LOVE

It's written in the stars:
the ocean of our love is real;
galaxies may come and go
but *our* love endures forever.

We may walk in many diverse shoes,
take wing thru infinite seasons,
rest for aons beneath the sands of time;
yet the colours of our forever love will never fade.

If silence filled the universe,
angels ceased their praise,
<u>our</u> song would rain diamonds
upon the placid naked air.

As the old universe grows dim,
<u>new</u> stars glisten in a peacock sky;
you and I tread fresh uncharted water,
garbed in everlasting robes of love.

As the Cosmos conceals herself,
we swim together in our mystic magic pool
and we are blessed
    caressed
      forever
        by our love
          our love
            our love...

©DMB.FB.(2013) (J)

WALK WITH ME

Walk with me
through the corridors of night;
Walk with me
till you see the Morning Light.

Walk with me
when the stars have all gone out;
Walk with me
when your world is filled with doubt.

Walk with me
when you've given all can give;
Walk with me
when you've lost the will to live.

Walk with me
when all your Dreams are tossed;
Walk with me
when all your Hope seems lost.

Walk with me
till your journey is complete;
Walk with me
and a Bright New Path you'll meet.

© 19-02-11   DMB.FB.J-C

THE DIVINE MYSTERY

Like a humming-bird in flight
barely visible, vibrating wings of light
you alighted, here in our world.

Your compassionate eye and beating heart,
golden song of tomorrow's new start
brought me into your smiling world.

You enchant, delight, warm, protect, give totally to me,
Your Love, a pure beacon, for all to see,
Since you descended from high to light my world.

I fell deeply in love with you,
you with a myriad of mystic ways;
Divine Majesty cloaked so none can see,
God-King, journey weary, Bravest as can be.

The Divine Mystery is YOU, my Beloved.

A HEAVENLY QUATRAIN
(Jesse)

Spring garden of new green bud growth,
Blossoms of exquisite new beauty,
are pale reflections of Heaven above,
and your mind, my Love.

© ACB.C. 14/06/2011

IF

If e'er my light grows pale & dim,
I'll never feel defeat,
because I know that *you'll* be there
still kneeling at my feet.

If e'er the world should turn away
with angry words above,
I know *you'll* hold me in your arms,
and sing your songs of love.

If e'er the beauty of my world
should fade or pass away,
your pure unblemished loveliness
would glorify my day.

If ever Darkness casts her cloak
to shadow where I roam,
I know *your* brilliant shining light
will guide me safely Home.

If ever at my Journey's end,
all else seems ended too,
I know *you'll* still be there, my love,
and my Heaven shall be with *you*.

©DMB.FB.   03-08-18   (JESSE TO C.)

LIFE'S DUET

Life is a duet
we both may sing,
for when I am with you
it is eternally Spring.

If all the world's flowers
were one lovely bouquet,
your beautiful presence
makes sweeter display.

If all of life's goodness
filled up the Earth,
your pure loving kindness
is trillion times worth.

Your bravery and valour
outshine heroes of old;
your loyal steadfastness
has never been told.

No words can describe
the awe that I feel
to be the receiver
of such love and such zeal.

I thank you <u>and</u> God
for your presence, my love;
You must be an Angel
sent from Heaven above.

God bless you, Beloved,
for all that you are
May together we reach
that unreachable Star.

Let us both sing together
Life's loving Duet;
thank the Power above us
that we two have met.

© DMB.FB. (02-12-14) JESSE-DAEMON TO C.

LOVE'S NEW BEGINNING

Your inner eyes are raining tears
and my heart's drowning in them.
let me mend your broken wing's
and joy become your Diadem.

A jewelled rainbow lights the sky
with sunlight through your tears
and Time rolls gently backward
to cancel wasted years

We return to our Beginning,
shards of the Past dissolve;
a fresh new start we're given,
my errors God absolves.

Come take my hand Beloved,
together we shall fly
unto a new Forever,
beyond the sapphire sky.

The crystal cup of morning breaks,
leaves diamond tears behind;
a new and glorious Dawn Awakes,
a better Path we find.

Now, Love Divine illuminates
the beautiful Pathway
that leads us both to reach at last
our Love-filled Golden Day.

© DMB.FBJ-C (2013) 20/09/13

OUR JOURNEY

I walk on Mother Earth
garbed in robes of clay
made threadbare by the falling years
and Time's relentless Day.

The walls of Mind protect
but form a prison cell
where precious seeds of heaven
are choked by weeds of hell.

The Hero's golden broom
sweeps the sand away
but open hole in roof
lets the mountain stay.

So still the chaos rises,
the mountain ever there;
it seems the task before us
is way beyond repair.

The whirlpool swallows Hope
and coughs up multi-fears,
but deep down in the centre,
a ray of Light appears.

The little urchin Joy
still sings his merry song,
while loving-kindness flows
from fingers frail but strong.

Our journey, hers and mine,
though weary, blurred and slow,
leads to a World Divine
blessed by God's holy Glow.

© DMB.FB. J (24-11-17)

"Eternal whispers from the cosmos,
of divine love and divine light,
via the late Fler Beaumont."

To M

I love you more than I love the fairest day of Spring
when flowers pastel forth and wild-birds sing,
I love you more than the sweetly falling rain,
I love you more than the air I breathe,
more than suns that shine, or moons that wane.

©1974. K.P.F.D.

M.
(FROM F.)

She is the perfect rose,
the precious gem
that blesses
the garden of the world,
breathing her sweetness
transforming this globe
into a paradise
beyond compare.

She is the gentle zephyr
whispering,
caressing the air
with tender loving sighs,
calming the raging tempest
bringing peace.

She is the song of Dawn,
a soft-eyed doe,
shedding halcyon rays.
She is the girl who sings
her own sweet song,
and wears the crown
of pure, eternal love.

©DMB (F-M). 11-10-71

SINCE YOU CAME INTO MY WORLD

Since you came into my world,
I have seen the sun,
breathed the perfume of the flowers,
and in the evening
when the day is done,
have heard the birds
in their leafy bowers.

Since you came into my world,
I have seen the moon,
I have heard the inner singing
of the stars,
felt the night's entrancing breezes cool,
and heard the gentle weaving
of the grass.

Since you came into my world,
I have seen the light
that shines from Heaven's portals
far above.

I have felt the beauty and delight;
for since you came into my world,
I have found love.

©DMB.FB. 29 AUGUST 1976 (F TO M)

DAEMON:
GOD, SPIRIT, ANGEL, PRINCE.

Angels never leave Heaven,
Angels like you
You're just a beautiful dream
I can't believe you're true.
You came from out of a blue sky,
You fill my life with your charms.
If Angels never leave Heaven
then how did you get in my arms ?

Dearest ONE do you know
How love so perfect still can grow?
And oft times it doth seem to me
Shall encompass the Earth,& bridge the sea

To lie with you & feel your touch,
Your love my darling means so much
A river lies within my core,
Of love, desire & passion- more.

The river leaps to meet with thee,
And pulsing both together, we
Find in our love a wondrous bond,
The ebb & flow of Nature's wand.
And so my darling, I will be
Your own true love eternally,
I'll stay forever by your side
My heart is yours whate'er betide.

© MEB 9 SEPTEMBER 1976 (M TO F & ☽)

THE ETERNAL DOOR

"FOR THE BELOVED IS THE TRULY BEAUTIFUL AND PERFECT, AND BLESSED (PLATO)

"AND SILVANUS WAS THERE, IN THE GLORY OF HEADGEAR, WITH WANDS OF WILLOW, FLOWER-CROWNED WITH LARGEST OF LILLIES." (VIRGIL)

Damon and Laelon

"LOVE IS OF IMMORTALITY" (PLATO)

LOVE POEMS FROM SPIRIT

"IN THE BEGINNING"

In the Beginning
the eternal Radiance quivered
and from its inner Core
of white purity
sprang the sublime Prince Laelon.

In the eternal second
it shimmered again
and from its diamond heart
sprang the Divine Prince Damon.

In the first Garden
they were united
and in their eternal eyes
shone Love, Beauty, Purity and Truth.

The Eden trees
whispered of their Presence,
and one leaf
shining with Dawn's pink glow
impelled itself
silently down
to kiss their sleeping clasped hands
and perhaps
sow the future seed
of their love and joining.

© ACB (2004) C.to Laelon and Damon

COME DAMON.
(MY BELOVED "TIGER")

Come, my love,
and we shall slink
through the jewelled night
parting emerald grass
and drinking from sapphire pools.

Our footsteps will be followed
by small paws
devotedly following
their wonderful Father of Cubs.

But we shall slink
quietly off together
to a hidden waterfall
where our love
will know no bounds.

When my love
is resting his Tiger eyes
I will tenderly
swish my pink tail
tantalising
over his beautiful body
till you stir
and pull me close again
and our days and nights
will become
a joyous glorious time
of never ending love.

©ACB (2000) C to Damon

"IN A TIME AND PLACE"

In a Time and Place
not of this world,
there is a green pool
where willows grace its shore;

Each flurry of breeze
scatters the white blossoms
and silver leaves
into scented boats
that glide on its quiet reflection.

The branches part
and my Love stands framed
in its green velvet.

His lily wreath gleams
in his pure silvern hair;
his covering with ancient clasp
swings and reveals
his lithe form,
and his beautiful smile
makes my heart race.

I don't want to break
the magic moment,
just capture the endless Morning
of looking into his eyes,
the window of his exquisite Soul.

"I love you", we whisper
and fold our arms
tenderly around each other
in endless embrace.

© ACB (2005) C.to Laelon

LOVELIEST OF LADIES

Loveliest of ladies,
my heart is yours,
and all I am,
Just you adores.

Within my heart
a dormant seed
sprang into life
when you agreed

to be my wife.
So fly with me
and be my love
endlessly.

21/12/04

©2004 DMB-FB-L

"THERE WOULD BE NO MORNING"

There would be no Morning
if you were not there
in my life.

Our love has become
an eternal Flame
that burns more brightly
and lights our future Path
each moment we share together.

Our first kiss
lit my soul
my heart soared
and I became eternally yours.

© ACB. (2005) C.to Damon and Laelon.

DAEMON

"DAEMON - GREAT SPIRIT HE INTERPRETS
BETWEEN GOD & MAN; THE MEDIATOR
WHO SPANS THE CHASM WHICH DIVIDES THEM,
AND IN HIM, ALL IS BOUND TOGETHER".

PLATO

11 EXTENDED HAIKU OF LOVE
(SYLLABLES = 5, 7, 5 + 5)

From the Eternal Lover to His Beloved
on the 11 levels of Being, and her response.

HOLY

Chi-Jesse to Chia

You, my Beloved,
are the Beginning and End
of my Quest Divine.
Forever, you're mine.

Chia to Chi-Jesse

The Divine Chi-Jesse
Breathes life into Chia
she dreams & awaits
their hearts entwined forever.

DIVINE

Daemon to C.

My C. my Queen,
your eyes shine with Love Divine
and so too do mine.
you are my Star-Queen.

C to Daemon.

Divine light, divine love,
millions of stars swirl
around your majestic mind
you are my beloved star-prince.

MATRIX

Damon to Chianti

Jewel-eyed Tigress;
emerald grass, sapphire pool,
Queen of the Jungle,
true Warrior Queen.

Chianti to Damon

Vivid blue eyes dazzling smile,
from jewelled, infinite possibilities world,
you are & always will be
my splendid, dearest, tiger- being to me.

MAGICAL

Laelon to Chirani

My Lovely Lady,
twice-born Indian maiden,
fine stamp of a woman
on a Bridge of Dreams.

Chirani to Laelon

Silvern hair, mystical smile
tower of strength, your calmness
and healing love surrounds me.
I am blest to have you near

ANGELIC

Angel to Angelle

Between us a Sword;
for another has my heart.
Yet there is a link:
We both are angels.
&
Between us a Sword;
I longed to give you comfort,
Touch you with my love;
So I became Two.

Angelle to Angel

I knew your silent watching,
I knew your need for me to stay,
from you, safety, kindness
as you tried to rectify the past.
&
You have my love, respect
and admiration always,
my thankfulness, golden angel.

HIDDEN

Justin to Chara.

You awoke my heart.
We sealed our love with twin rings
of sweet plaited grass.
A cave's our Heaven.

Chara to Justin.

Justin, my darling love,
your strength, our rings,
our cave
you lit my world with your love.
It is truly eternally returned.

SPIRITUAL

Jolyon to Juliette

Our spirits soar free
to our own enchanted land
on crystalline wings
upheld by Pure Love.

Juliette to Jolyon

You were the hidden one
who managed to survive,
and move thru other minds,
and <u>how</u> I do love thee.
It is with all my heart and soul.

ASTRAL

Jesse-Daemon to Old She

Old witch with Cauldron,
If no-one else existed,
<u>you</u> would be enough.
I'm under your Spell.

Old She to Daemon

My young man calls me
astride my broom I fly through
the starry night to be beside
together, forever in everlasting love.

FAERY

Demon to Mab

Dark Queen of the Night
Black thoughts weave into minds, dreams;
All's not what it seems:
Faery- glamour rules.

Damon to Mab

Our love may combust,
return us to dust
or it may ignite
return us to Light.
Mab to Damon. P.183

PHYSICAL

Azaziel to J

Like a diamond bright
you sparkled into my life
redeeming my Soul
and making me whole.

J. to Azaziel

Your smile & wit disarmed me
it called my sleeping mind awake
drawing me to your side, &
I thank heaven we met, love.

DARK SPHĔRES

Damon to Mab

Our love may combust,
return us to dust
or it may ignite
return us to Light.

MAB TO DAMON

In the purple darkness
my love stands silently,
watching and unfazed,
together we can achieve
our loving destiny

© DMB.FB. (2013) D.
© AB (2013) M.

6 HAIKU to the Retinue
& their reply to *Daemon*

Phaedra, you're the Peach
that never loses its glow.
I desire you so!

                    You have the power, love
                    to make me anything,
        with enduring love and desire.
                                Phaedra

Old She: Witch Supreme,
let us both fly together
through your darksome Woods.

                    My young man calls
                    we fly together
            through star studded skies.
                                Old She

Laura, I love you
your lovely country Cottage
is my pure Haven.

                    Cottage bakes on sill
        welcomes your divine prescence
                        into my life.
                                Laura

Jael, my Shining Knight
Let us ride to your Castle
on our gallant steeds..

            Flag flying from castle turret
              proclaiming my love and
                  allegiance to you.
                                Jael

Dryal, Timeless One
We swim in your Sea-Kingdom
Riding Sea-Horses.

          Sand and foam, diamond sea
                    starlight Being
                      be here with me.
                                Dryal

Marcel, Mon Ami,
let us stroll in your Chateau,
sharing Love and Wine.

          Warm croissants, french coffee
                 under our tree, just
vous et moi, all Mon Coeur and Amour.
                                Marcel

---

to all from Daemon.

How I do love thee!
Each one a rare and precious Gem
In my Princely Diadem.

©16-10-2013

5 HAIKU
(Daemon to Retinue) & their reply to him

TO FAFNIR
Fafnir, mighty one,
I'll dance with you,
to the wings of song.

FROM FAFNIR
Dance with me,
over land and sea
just us together, eternally.

TO ELLIE
You captured my heart
With your magic silken rope
And tied a Love-knot.

FROM ELLIE
This lady has a rope,
You
closer to me
is my hope,
you have my heart
in a love-knot

TO THE WHOLE RETINUE
I am truly blessed
to have such wondrous Love
from my Retinue.

My fine Retinue
to the strains of winged song
you follow me home.

My Love enfolds All;
as your Love blesses me,
We shall never part.

© DMB. D.F.B. (Nov 2013)

TO PRINCE DAEMON
(FROM THE RETINUE)

From every dimension down
we saw your Light emerge
from that distant Tunnel.

Fully cloaked,
we still knew
you were there.

Drawn to your side
we came
offering our deep love.

Time has made no difference
to our hearts;
it only made our love stronger.

We stand by your side,
our vows of love
to just you.

We follow forever
your everlasting Star-Light
to an eternity
with your Divine Presence.

It is our Happy-Ever-After.

©F.B. RET-P1-P2 (2013)

"For me, shall it become all things,
and upon it's light, the World
will rise to greet my coming day.
The song unsung, shall find it's hidden chord,
and in the marble hand of time,
the bowl will break freeing,
scattering, the secret flowers
that lit my former way."

Earthbound. 11/10/71
P.Mardon (SEER)

CHRISTMAS HILLS

THE OLD COUNTRY SCHOOL
(MEMORIES OF CHRISTMAS HILLS)

In a little country school
down a leafy lane so cool
we children loved to run and chase and play;
we'd play hopscotch, hide-and-seek,
cool off down in the creek
when it was hot and dusty summer day.

There was cricket, leap-frog too,
and when the sky was blue
we'd swing beneath a big old friendly tree;
we'd play marbles on the ground,
chase each other round and round;
we were all as free and happy as could be.

Using branches as our brooms
we made pine-needles into rooms,
while the wildbirds sang above us merrily;
we rolled rusty old iron hoops,
knitted sox and sweaters for the troops
as we sat on sweet green grass beneath a tree.

On hot summer days we drank
from an outdoor water tank
which in winter time would gently overflow.
Yes well do I remember
from Feb. until December
those days of over sixty years ago.

* * * * * * *

Fler Beaumont © 2000.

THE MOPOKE
(A TRUE STORY OF THE 1940s)

'Twas a hot summer's day
when she ambled our way,
Old Becky who wandered our Hills.
She sat 'neath our tree,
Drank and sang merrily.
Ah! My mind with her memory fills.

Mum gave her sandwich and tea
which she ate gratefully
as she rested beneath the gum tree.
From then, every night,
as the stars shone so bright,
a mopoke's hoot filled the air eerily.

We started to wonder
if the tree Beck sat under
was not just her shelter by day;
but maybe at night
she transformed and took flight
as a mopoke, and sheltered that way.

In Autumn Beck died;
Ah, yes! how we cried.
We placed flowers where Becky had lain
'neath the big old gum tree.
Now her spirit was free
we never heard mopoke again.

©DIANA MARY BATES (2014)

FLOWER-CHILD

I was a flower-child
of the sixties;
not into drugs or sex,
but pure true love
for everyone everything
caring sharing promoting peace.
Donovan and Dylan sang their songs.

I wore a flower in my hair,
love in my heart.
Myself a traumatized child,
I gave refuge to another;
fed the hungry cat, hugged a tree,
singing songs of love and writing poetry.
A Brotherhood of man and beast and tree.

The remnant from that time
was lasting love for all.
The sheltered child
became a gift from God:
the caring and the sharing that I gave
flowed back from her
to bless and heal my life.

No matter now
how hard the blow
the pain the fear the strife,
within the centre of my soul
there lives the golden glow
of love for her and God
and gratitude for life.

©DMB.F.BJ 23-10-14

IN TRYING TIMES

These are trying times for sure;

those once so rich are now so poor.
But let us through these lessons grow
in spirit, love, compassion. So,
although our portion may be small,
let us, with kindness, share with all.

A fellow-feeling, once so rare,
has gripped us as we learn to share
our meagre portion with another,
once a stranger, now a brother.
Perhaps these times are but a test
to make us do our very best.

Who knows but 'tis God's master-plan
to help us love our fellow-man?
What better way than empathy
with those unfortunate as we?
So do not fret nor anger show,
but take this chance to learn and grow.

© DMB.FB 1993

THE TIME OF BLUE HYACINTHS

Hyacinth,
you saw the child of clay
the out-of-focus eyes
the twisted turned-in feet
and scrabbling hands
the tangled mind
that knew not who or why or where
but trapped within the cave
of its own peculiar insularity
saw only shadows on the wall.

Outside
Spring had come
bestowing rich enchantment;
but within the cave
she was not known;
the child still dwelled
within a time of its own.

Hyacinth,
you came
small green fingers
struggling upward
to absorb the pallid light
that filtered through the cave.
The child
misunderstood the gift
and smote with fearful fists
the tender shoot.
Still you endured.

Spring advanced;
your beauty was revealed
in a miracle of blue.
It held the child's mute gaze
stilled the tangled mind.
no longer out-of-focus
it now knew who it was,
the why and where.

Hyacinth,
love crystallized between the child and you.
Within the glorious incandescence
of Beauty, Truth and Love
two souls merged
their Spirits set free
upon the wings of Eternity.

And the time of blue hyacinths
had passed.

****

Dedicated to my beautiful foster-daughter and friend
Andrea who taught me the true meaning of life,
love, compassion, endurance, forgiveness and giving,
She brought Light into my life.

Fler Beaumont © 2003.

NIGHT SKY AT CHRISTMAS HILLS

Evening crept gently over the quiescent hills
and the wild-birds ceased their song.
The air lay hushed
as the sky darkened to indigo.

The gilded goblet of the crescent moon
embraced the brilliant evening star
as they slipped over the far horizon
on their nightly tryst.

In the now sable sky
tiny scintillas of light began to emerge
until the night sky
was drenched with glittering stars.

Only the friendly hoot
of old Mopoke
high up in the big gum tree
nudged the silence of the night.

And all the land below
lay kissed with soft starlight.

©Diana Mary Bates (2010)

MIND MAGIC

In Mind's realm is neither time nor space;
we may dwell in distant past or future mist;no longer
bound to this our solar place,
we wander in the Cosmos, full of bliss.

The season's spell is shattered and we see
Snowdrops, not in Winter but in Fall.
The rose's gentle perfume we perceive,
and *other* Seasons hold us in their thrall.

All that ever was, is with us now,
And all that is to come, we know in full.
For Spirit does the human mind endow
With powers far beyond the earthly pull.

The Mind is never prisoner of the clay;
it's essence never was of lower caste.
Within its realm is more than night and day,
more than present, future and the past.

Yes, we may leave our bodies and thus find
we are not bound in fetters or in chains;
we really are the ever-present Mind
which dance to sweet other -world refrains.

© DMB - FB. 1993

REALITY

Come walk with me
in the world of Reality.
Don't be lured into self-ish insularity
in the world of Imagination
in which there is no real creation;
it is illusion, maya,
a trap
from which there is no salvation.

Imagination
is not a PLACE to be;
it is a TOOL
that we can use
to create a better Reality
for you and me.

Be a *real* hero
in the *real* world.
Create hope and joy
and real love to share
with real people there.
Let Reality shine
with it's Light Divine.
Fulfil your own true destiny
and you'll really be free.

© DMB. FB.J 10-08-15

COUNSEL FOR THE OLD & FRAIL

Do not fear the counsel of the years;
it does not mean your life's about to end.
we all are blessed with sunshine and with tears;
we would not grow without this wholesome blend.

As the old clay coat we wear grows pale and thin,
and all the threads that bind begin to break,
so now awakes the Spirit from within
aware that soon old customs must forsake.

When all the *outer* clamour fades away,
we turn *within* and find a treasure rare:
an inner glow which guides and lights our way,
serenity and peace beyond compare.

So do not mourn for loss of sight nor sound,
nor for the lost control of hands and feet;
for in their absence, you have truly found
that which makes your journey more complete.

We then shall rise and greet the Newborn Day
with vision clear and music sweetly heard;
true clarity and strength come into play;
We'll wing and sing like Heaven's joyous Bird.

© DMB. FB. L. (5/4/13)

IF WINTER COMES...

Winter has crept into my house
on soft silent slippered feet
and caught me unawares.
Where did Autumn go?

I search for her
in empty vaults and cupboards;
dust and cobwebs everywhere.
No time to sweep or clean.

The minute hand is poised
to meet the midnight hour
and the hour-glass is almost spent.
Memory struggles beneath the weight of fallen sand.

The tooth-fairy has departed
with her purse devoid of silver coins.
Chatter has ceased
and smiling faces gone.

One single fading flower remains.
But ah! the beauty and the fragrance
of that one flower
outweighs the world of wealth gone by.

Weak and weary limbs relax,
accept the councel of the years.
An unexpected gift appears
to chase away the rising fears.

Continued...

These two most lovely gifts from God
now lift my spirit
warm my hearth
and joy returneth home
.
Ther darkening sky becomes awash with stars
as love, hope, comfort wrap me round.
True peace of mind and soul
have now been found.

Now re-awakens Autumn, Summer, Spring
within my heart
and I give thanks to God
for this New Start.

© DMB. FBJ. 10/ 28-01-16
Dedicated to Andrea (the Flower) and Paul (the Gift)

THE LADY OF THE STARS

She came from the stars.
Her beauty, beyond anything seen on Earth,
could have launched
a thousand *million* space-ships.

Translucent skin,
lit from within;
eyes, twin pools of midnight,
bright with stars.

Grace beyond compare,
she raised one slender hand
and it seemed
that all the glories of the Universe

cascaded down
like a shimmering waterfall
of radiant splendour,
blessing the ground whereon she stood.

Her smile dispelled all fear,
awakened unparalleled bliss.
The moment hung suspended
like crystal in the air.

When she left,
returning to the stars from which she came,
it was as though
all light had left the world.

Yet...
Upon the ground where she had stood,
there lingered a soft glimmering glow
shot with glittering stars...

© Fler Beaumont a.k.a Diane Mary Bates, June 2007

January 3, 2015

Fler Beaumont
Victoria, Australia

Dear Jesse, - Fler,

I've just read all your poems, and I was mightily impressed by them! Truly. They seem to have been divinely inspired. Makes me think that you were actually taken over by some kind of afflatus. I much prefer your version of creation to that of the astrophysicists and cosmologists. All of your poems seemed to emanate from the same Source, but the one I particularly responded to was God's Song. If you had a laminated version of that, I would affix it somewhere in my house for friends to read. I also wonder if you have thought of putting out a little book of these poems. If so, I would love to have a copy. Anyway, they were very moving for me to read. You have the gift, all right.

Love, Ken
Kenneth Ring, P.H.D, Author of *'Lessons of the Light'*.

Ken and Fler

'Afflatus' communication of Supernatural knowledge - Divine Inspiration. (Concise Oxford Dictionary - 1934.)

ABOUT THE AUTHOR

1998
IANDS - AUSTRALIA
Australian chapter of the International Association for Near-Death Studies Inc.
Victoria 3056, Australia.

President: Fler Beaumont
Vice-President: Andrea Beaumont
Director of Counselling: Sylvia Eriksson
Newsletter: "LIGHT"

This resignation of Fler's winds up her 12 years of tireless work in the Near-Death field. It covers her support at the inaugural meeting of Australiands (Melbourne Branch) then her establishment of Victoriands, founding editorship of 3 newsletters *(Light, Quanta, Victoriands)*. She then went on to establish the I.A.N.D.S. Melbourne Research division, became State host and organiser of the Dr Peter Fenwick and Professor Kenneth Ring Australia tours, and Founding President of I.A.N.D.S. Australia. This was an enormous workload for a cancer patient and included lectures, meetings, enquiries, interviews, hospice and library tapes, workshops, seminars, articles, providing secondary N.D.E. research, and collating and writing her own 2 N.D.E. books. Unfortuantely these will now have to be finished at a later date. Her work was fuelled by her own N.D.E.'s & "the need to uplift & share her knowledge with others.". We thank you dear Fler, for <u>ALL</u> you have contributed to the spreading of the spiritual message of the near-death experience and for spreading the message of unconditional love and light to this waiting world.

Rev. S. Eriksson
Director of Counselling - Publicity Officer
I.A.N.D.S. Australia

100% of profits of this book are going to Animals Australia. Available on Amazon 2021

'To know even one life has breathed easier because you have lived. This is to have succeeded.'

In Fler Beaumont, the animals have lost a cherished friend and advocate. Fler's path has forged a kinder future for those who share this world with us. Through the spirit of kindness and compassion, her legacy lives on.

SOURCES AND ACKNOWLEDGEMENTS

These are sincerely made, for the following individuals and publishers, for the use of certain itemised contents in this volume. If anyone has been accidentally overlooked, the next publishing will correct this oversight.

1.(a) - Front cover photo-Craig Sillitoe on assignment for 'The Age-Life'.

(b) - Kind permission-By Sebastian Liistro for use of the image of his residence for the front cover photo.

Dedication page

2.(a) - 'Ubi caritas' - Early Gregorian chant-France. (Mannix library-Catholic Archdiocese Melb).

2.(b) - 'There is nothing holier in this life'-Henry Wadsworth Longfellow-Hyperion p.215. 1887. G. Routledge & Sons.

2.(c) - And at the touch of love-Plato (The Dialogues of Plato-1875 p.47.B.Jowett Oxford Clarendon Press.)

A special grateful acknowledgement to Paul Sandalis for the caring and original typing of Flers' poems and wonderful assistance with copyright searches.

P.2. Coloured star plates ,(including p.2, p.44, p.104, p.119, p.164, p.168, p.174, p.182 and back cover) by kind permission of Keith P. Cooper-Pole Star Publication LTD. UK. 2006. (Astronomy- The Grand Tour of the Universe.)

P.3. Iamblichus - Translation by Thomas Taylor, - 'Iamblichus on mysteries of the Egyptians Chaldean's & Assyrians'. 1821 1st edition. P.301 & P.343. C. Whittingham. Cheswick.

P.24. Permission is granted for "THIS LITTLE BIRD" written by JOHN LOUDERMILK 1965, © Sony/atv acuff rose music. Licenced by Sony Music Publishing (Australia) P/L. International Copyright secured. All rights Reserved. Used by permission.

P.27. 'In God we Live'. (St James Bible with concordence, Acts 17. V.28. Oxford Uni. Press G Cumberlege. London. 1953.)

P.39. 'All praise be to God' (St James Bible with concordence, Acts 17. V. 28. Oxford Uni. Press G Cumberlege. London. 1953.) & John chapter 13. verse 34.

P.43. Iamblichus - Translation by Thomas Taylor, - 'Iamblichus on mysteries of the Egyptians Chaldean's & Assyrians'. 1821 1st edition. P.301 & P.343. C. Whittingham. Cheswick.

P.44. 'For God mingles not with man'. (The Dialogues of Plato, P.54, translated by B.Jowett.)(1817-1893) (Front page) Oxford Clarendon Press. 1875. (back cover, Mac Millan & Co. 1875)

P.60. 'As Diatima, the mantian sibyl said to Socrates.'
'Love is the blessedest God.' (P.46.)
'Love is of the everlasting.' (P.58.)
(The Dialogues of Plato, translates by B.Jowlett (1817-1899)
Oxford Clarendon Press 1875

P.104. 'Love overmastereth all' - Virgil. (The Eclogues of Virgil - Sir Geogre O. Morgan. 1826-1899) Henry Fowde. 1897.

P.119. 'Lover take my hand' (P.Mardon. 9-2-73)

P.164. 'I love you, more than I love.' (P.Mardon. 1974)

P.168. 'For the beloved'- Plato. (The Dialogues of Plato.)   (Translated by B.Jowett. 1817-1893) Oxford Clarendon Press 1875. P.55

P.168. 'And Silvanus was there'. (The Eclogues of Virgil. P.46. Sir. G.O. Morgan 1826-1897.)

P.168. 'Love is of immortality'- Plato. (The Dialogues of Plato.) (Translated by B.Jowett 1817-1893) Oxford Clarendon Press 1875.

P.174. 'Daemon' - "Great spirit, he interprets between God and man;" - Plato. P.54. (The Dialogues of Plato. (Translated by B.Jowett 1817-1893) Oxford Clarendon Press 1875.

P.182. 'For me, shall it become all things' 'Earthbound' P.Mardon. 11/10/71.

P.196. 'Afflatus'- Communication of Supernatural Knowledge. (Divine Inspiration). The Concise Oxford Dictionary. 2nd edition. P.22. 1934. H.W.Fowler.

Sincere and grateful acknowledgement to Kenneth Ring, Established Author, for his encouraging letter, use of photo, and enduring friendship.

P.197. About the author. -IANDS Australia.1998.
Grateful acknowledgement to Rev. S. Eriksson. I.A.N.D.S. Australia

P.198. Memorium page - Animals Australia. 5/9/2019 Brenda Curran and team. (100% of profits of this book to them.)

P.199. Sources and Acknowledgement pages. Also grateful acknowledgement to the following generous individuals, whose patience and assistance I deeply valued while compiling this book.

Andrew McConville - State Library Victoria.

Lisa Gerber - Mannix Library.

Angeletta Leggio - Baillieu Library.

APRA-Amcos team - Jenny Branagan, Glen Bennie.

Phoebe Ponder - Sony Music Publishing (Australia) P/L.

Blaise Van Hecke and team - Busybird Publishing.

Daniela Da Pozzo - Office support.

Alex Salpietro - Publishing Consultant.

Pamela Coutts - Author.

www.ingramcontent.com/pod-product-compliance
Lightning Source LLC
Chambersburg PA
CBHW041957080526
44588CB00021B/2769